THE BROADCAST
JOURNALISM HANDBOOK

THE BROADCAST JOURNALISM HANDBOOK

A Television News Survival Guide

ROBERT THOMPSON
and
CINDY MALONE

ROWMAN & LITTLEFIELD PUBLISHERS, INC.
Lanham • Boulder • New York • Toronto • Oxford

ROWMAN & LITTLEFIELD PUBLISHERS, INC.

Published in the United States of America
by Rowman & Littlefield Publishers, Inc.
A wholly owned subsidiary of The Rowman & Littlefield Publishing Group, Inc.
4501 Forbes Boulevard, Suite 200, Lanham, Maryland 20706
www.rowmanlittlefield.com

P.O. Box 317, Oxford OX2 9RU, United Kingdom

Figures appear courtesy of Kelly Quiring, Kelly Design Group.

British Library Cataloging in Publication Information Available

Library of Congress Cataloging-in-Publication Data

Thompson, Robert, 1962–
    The broadcast journalism handbook : a television news survival guide /
Robert Thompson and Cindy Malone.
        p.   cm.
    Includes bibliographical references and index.
    ISBN 0-7425-2505-8 (Cloth : alk. paper) — ISBN 0-7425-2506-6
(Paper : alk. paper)
    1. Television broadcasting of news—Vocational guidance.   2. Broadcast
journalism—Vocational guidance.   I. Malone, Cindy, 1964–   II. Title.
PN4784 .T4T48   2004
070.1'95—dc21   2003008692

Printed in the United States of America

∞™ The paper used in this publication meets the minimum requirements of
American National Standard for Information Sciences—Permanence of Paper for
Printed Library Materials, ANSI/NISO Z39.48-1992.

This book is dedicated to Shirley Ross.

With each serving of eggs and cheeses,
coffee and bagels . . . you became
our inspiration and our friend.
Thank you for everything!

Love,
Cindy & Robert

CONTENTS

Foreword   ix
Introduction   xi

1 TV News: The Myth and the Reality   1
2 You've Got the Job, What Do You Do Now?   9
3 Your First Day   17
4 Putting It All Together: Cast and Crew   29
5 Newsroom Survival Guide   43
6 The Business of News   59
7 Crossing the Line   71
8 One-Man Bands   79
9 The Story   85
10 Where to Go, What to Do, Who to Call?   99
11 Making Deadlines   113
12 Writing Tips   119
13 Into Practice   135
14 News Quiz: Test Your Knowledge of History,
   Recent Events, and People   143
15 Worst-Case Scenarios   147
16 Amateur Errors   153
17 Getting the Job   161
18 Wrap-Up   165

Appendix A: Going Online   171
Appendix B: About the Journalists Interviewed   175

News Glossary   179
Index   187
About the Authors   191

FOREWORD

All of the examples used in this book are true. They really happened. They are compilations by the authors of events and incidents that actually happened to them or to the many seasoned journalists that gave of their extremely precious personal time to contribute to this book. Nothing can teach better than real experience and what others learned from it.

INTRODUCTION

WHAT'S REAL

Oh my God! This isn't how it was supposed to be!" Instead of New York City and the *Today* show, it's Laredo, Texas, (market 200-something) and the show-me-what-to-do. Instead of Washington, D.C., and the *NewsHour with Jim Lehrer,* it's Great Falls, Montana, and I-never-learned-that-in-college.

It turns out that television news doesn't go by the book. On one hand, it's fractured and frenzied, illogical and unfair. On the other, it's a job where every day at work is a new experience, a new chance to learn . . . and what we've learned is that, in three easy steps, we can help make your first real job in your first real newsroom a real success.

Step 1: Remember everything you learned in college journalism.

Step 2: Forget everything you learned in college journalism.

Step 3: Read this book. It's full of things you didn't learn in class and things an internship could never teach . . . tips that will help you stand out in the newsroom and on air. We're giving you a head start. Take it.

WHAT TO DO

Imagine yourself at your first job in a small market in the Midwest, Des Moines, Iowa, perhaps. You turn on the TV on your day off to watch the morning news programs. The world has turned upside down. Two planes have crashed into the world's most prominent buildings, the World Trade Center. A plane has crashed into the United States's most stalwart defense, the Pentagon. Reports are that yet another plane, possibly others, are hijacked and may be heading for Washington, D.C., or the West Coast. News is breaking constantly. What goes through your mind? What do you do?

- Do nothing, stay in bed, keep watching.
- Call some friends in New York to find out what's happening; you can't get through.
- Call the newsroom.
- Head in to work.

There's no true right or wrong answer here, but your response can help you gauge how you feel about being a newsperson. In this case, most journalists would either call work, or just head on in, knowing they would be there for a long time and wanting to contribute.

When you get to work, your news director is busy monitoring the network to find out if your newscasts are preempted and exactly how much local time the networks are willing to give up at this point. You're on your own and must assume that all newscasts will go on as scheduled. You don't have a story scheduled, and the early reporter is still out on a shoot set up before the attacks, so there's no one to turn to. What do you do?

- Watch TV network coverage.
- Make local calls, see what other news is going on locally.
- Check the assignment desk calendar and follow up on what's already scheduled for today.
- Start checking out how your town is reacting, think of local angles to the greater story.

You need to be doing something and you need to stay informed about events across the country. Before seeing how people are reacting, it is important to keep up on what's going on nationally, as this is a changing story. If you have a noon newscast, go out and get local folks' reaction. Is there a military installation in the area? Make the call and talk to the PIO (public information officer). Are they on heightened alert? Find out the most you can, then hit the streets, constantly monitoring the national situation. How many story ideas can you come up with on this first day? Here are some of ours.

Local reaction, MOS's (man on the street).

Anyone locally connected, or anyone local know any victims?

Nationally asking for blood donations . . . how's the local blood bank doing?

Are malls, other public places shut down?

What about other sponsored events, any cancellations? People need to know.

Anyone locally raising money for the cause, or planning to?

Any military or rescue personnel on standby to head to New York or D.C.?

Go to the local university and talk to professors—they may have experts in aviation, terrorism, and psychology.

Talk to local psychologists; how are people reacting, how can people work their way through such a tragedy, and how can they help explain this to their kids?

Head to the airport, talk to stranded passengers.

Talk to the local car rental places, Greyhound Bus, and Amtrak, to find out if they are becoming booked up.

Talk to local city officials. Any contingency plans in place for a mass disaster, or for security measures?

Are people going to local churches for comfort?

These are just some of the possible local angles. You'll most likely, as a reporter in a small market, or an assignment desk person or writer in a larger market, be on your own in thinking up story ideas and taking charge.

Of course, a story like this comes along maybe a few times in a journalist's career, but these are the times that test your skills, abilities, responsibilities, and success as a broadcast newsperson. Are you up to the task? Days like this can change lives, and the responsibility on you as the messenger of the news is daunting, and at times, sobering. That's why you need to be as prepared as possible to take charge. This could have been *your* first day at work. We'll help you get ready for it.

STOP, LOOK, LISTEN, AND REMEMBER

Wondering if news is for you? You're not alone. Sprinkled throughout this handbook you'll find what we like to call "Newsbites." They are thoughts, experiences, anecdotes, and advice . . . from TV news professionals. (The Newsbites appear in boxes that are shaded gray.) People who asked and continue to ask themselves the same question: *Is news for me?* Some stories will inspire, some will leave you laughing, some may even scare you, but never fear. We include them for a reason, to be a voice from the void. Read them now. Flag your favorites. Refer back to them when you need that extra boost of news knowhow or when you just need to remind yourself why news is what you chose.

THE JOB

"I love the fact that reporting and anchoring have allowed me to experience so many different things in life. How many accountants get to . . .

- Meet the president.
- Fly a fighter jet.
- Expose a crook.
- Give views on life to a gym full of school kids.
- Climb Mount Rushmore.
- Hang out of a helicopter with a camera.
- Travel to a Third World country.
- Help a child find caring parents.
- Drive a real tank.
- Make someone's day by remembering their name?"

Tom Hanson, anchor

"What I like about my job . . . I don't know about love . . . is that my job changes every day. Also, my job keeps me up on current events."

Scott Jordan, videotape editor

"The thing I love about it is meeting people, being in their environment—no one ever comes to the TV station to have their story told, you have to go to them. I also love the art of framing good shots, getting sequences, and telling stories. My motto is 'everyone has a story to tell, my job is to shut up and let them tell it.'"

Carol Lynde, photographer

"If it's a struggle to read the paper every morning and you don't particularly want to know how your government and city works . . . you're in the wrong job."

Jim Hanchett, anchor

"I love being an editor because it keeps me up to date on current events and things going on around the world. I see video before anyone else sees it and some video that never airs. I love the creativity that comes along with the fancy system that we have to edit on. We can create clips of video by adding effects and colors and other pieces of video."

Janine White, videotape editor

THE PAY

"I cleared something like $325 every two weeks and my rent was $375 a month. I remember wearing my college polo shirts on the air and buying groceries at a gas station so I could put them on a gas credit card."

Sarah Pooler, former reporter/anchor

THE LAUGHS

"I was so nervous on one live shot in Colorado Springs, I mispronounced my last name! I laughed it off and kept going! Small mistakes don't have to be acknowledged."

Debbie Denmon, anchor

THE PERKS

"It has permitted me to travel the world with an excuse to nose around about matters that I find interesting. This is a profession for people always interested in learning . . . often firsthand."

Michael Moffett, freelance producer

THE REALITY

"One must be aggressive, outgoing, and willing to keep going even when encountering *no* at every turn. I thought my duty was to change the world and make a huge difference with every story. That only happens in a dream world. Now, I look for moments of opportunity."

Dan Lothian, correspondent, NBC

Speaking of opportunity, it's knocking. Let's see if we can help you make the most of it.

1

TV NEWS: THE MYTH AND
THE REALITY

THE MYTH

You are an intern at one of the leading TV stations in the country, big market news. As soon as you graduate, the news director offers you an on-air reporting position for $50,000 a year. Two months later, you are the only reporter in the station when a huge breaking news story happens. No one's around to do the cut-ins, so you have to anchor the coverage. The general manager of the station sees you and wants you to replace the main anchor. But you turn her down because Tom Brokaw was in town that day, saw you anchor, and has demanded that NBC offer you a network job making seven figures. At this point, all you need to worry about is if you'll like your wardrobe, hair, and makeup stylists, and how to spend all your money.

Wake up!! If only it were that easy. Instead, the TV news business will be a career full of rocky times, great moments, possibly dangerous situations, and mostly long and odd hours, hard work, and low pay. That's why you need to make sure you jump in with both feet,

---

"It's very unforgiving. It's not fun if it is just a job, it has to become part of you, because this career becomes your life and demands personal sacrifice."

Patti Dennis, news director

---

and why you need to love this work, because at times it can be one of the most thankless of all jobs. If you think you're ready for it, read on.

THE NEWSROOM: THE REALITY

If you had an internship, you may have some idea of what it's like to work in a TV newsroom. Probably the overwhelming impression is: chaos! A former college student with an internship in a major market once asked how everyone knew what was going on, and how anything got done. Good question! We, too, thought it was chaotic because we didn't quite understand the newsgathering process. But we soon learned that the chaos is just built in . . . it's inherent in the system. Everyone is working separately, on their own tasks, yet somehow working together to complete the whole . . . the TV newscast.

cha·os, \\'kā-,äs\ *n.* a state of complete disorder and confusion; a television newsroom
chap, \\'chap\ *v.* **chapped, chapping,** split; roughen

A day in the life of anyone in a newsroom, whether it's the assignment editor, producer, reporter, anchor, photographer, editor, or news manager, is chaotic, stressful, and oftentimes frantic. Many times, it's hurry-up-and-wait, and much of the time spent at work is time spent under a lot of pressure. And it's rare when someone thanks you at the end of the workday. There isn't a whole lot of glamour involved in doing a story on city council's newest ordinance, or answering phone calls from angry viewers (usually about programming decisions that have nothing to do with the newsroom), or writing

"My internship made me understand what it takes to get news on TV. After six months, I was even editing!"
Chris Berg, news director

five-second teases. Even street reporting turns into a daily grind at times. Be prepared for this. Of course, spot news spices up life in the newsroom, but it doesn't happen every day. So, why would anyone want to continue in this job? It sounds so thankless, and let's face it, the pay is very low, until you reach a major market (and not everyone there makes a great salary, either). Simple: you love your job, you love telling stories, and you want to make a difference. As a bonus, you work against the clock, so there's no time sitting around an office, waiting to go home; there's certainly no time to get bored!

RECIPE FOR SUCCESS

What does it take to make it in this environment? For the most part, a willingness to work a lot of hours, on any shift, at any time. And you need to be comfortable with change . . . the story you talk about in the assignment meeting almost always changes once you get out into the field. Or the entire newscast you produced all day long can go out the window when breaking news happens. As an assignment editor, you'll have to drop setting up that story for the afternoon reporter to

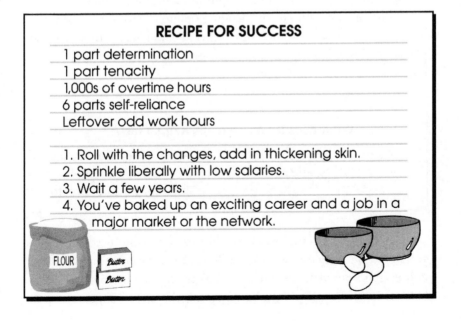

RECIPE FOR SUCCESS

1 part determination
1 part tenacity
1,000s of overtime hours
6 parts self-reliance
Leftover odd work hours

1. Roll with the changes, add in thickening skin.
2. Sprinkle liberally with low salaries.
3. Wait a few years.
4. You've baked up an exciting career and a job in a major market or the network.

FLOUR   Butter   Butter

chase that spot news. Change is built in, and the faster you can adapt to changing conditions and formulate quick solutions, the better off you'll be.

Thinking on your feet is invaluable, too. Stories can present themselves in any place and in many forms, so you always need to be on the lookout. News is constantly a challenge of a fixed workload with very limited resources, so quick and creative thinking will serve you well, especially in the eyes of management.

Stick to your principles. Listen to yourself. Even if everyone else is taking close-up shots of the crumpled body of a rock climber who fell to his death, and your photographer did too, maybe you don't feel the need to air that shot. You don't feel it adds to the story. Later, as the editor is putting that shot into the story, you hear scanner traffic of a possible heart attack victim. You hear the dispatcher say it's the wife of the rock climber, apparently in shock after she got the news of her husband's death. The editor thinks that's not a reason to leave out the shot. You, as the producer, do. You insist that the shot be edited out. The editor argues that these things happen every day and it's not a big deal; don't be so sensitive. You, as the producer, are ultimately responsible for what airs, and you insist again that the shot be removed. You'll get flak, but you feel you did the right thing in this instance.

You will constantly be exchanging opinions with other individuals in the newsroom, sometimes pleasantly, and many times not so pleasantly. Listen to others' opinions, especially seasoned individuals, but do what you think is right, too.

What does it take to make it in TV news?

"Passion for what you do. Otherwise the obstacles like low pay, long hours, and a frantic work pace are insurmountable."
Chris Berg, news director

Respect other employees' workloads. Everyone is stressed, but you're not the only one with a deadline. Don't start chatting with the editor after you write your story, if he's trying to edit your story and half of the show, too. If you're done, ask the editor if you can pull some file video for him and cue it up. Just because you're done with your part of the workload doesn't mean the news day is over. Watching TV, surfing the web, or making personal phone calls until the end of your shift isn't in your job description.

Handle stress. Bottom line—if you can't handle stress or at least can't work under severe stressful conditions, then this career isn't for you. You will be faced with stressful circumstances just about every day of your working career. It comes with the territory. Some folks actually work better under a lot of stress.

Be thrifty. With few exceptions, you're not going to make any money for a while. Enough said.

> "Don't expect it to be easy being on television. So many people think there is no work involved in being a good journalist, and that being on television is easy. It's not."
> Hayley Herst, assignment manager

Have a support system—whether it's your parents, friends, or significant other, it's good to have someone to support your goals and to help you out financially while you're struggling in a small market. This is where those care packages from parents can really come in handy! These can be lifesavers.

And let's face it, TV news is stressful on adult relationships. You're not really going to make your way up the ladder in a small market. You may go from reporter to anchor, but the only way to move up is to move out, to another market, another station, another city altogether. If you're married, your spouse needs to know this and accept this from the get-go.

Be sensitive to the politics of the station and the town you're working in. This may seem at times to go against your principles, but you always need to gauge the environment. In essence, you need to fit in, while trying to stand out in a crowd. It's a real juggling act at times. If you're working in a very staunch, conservative market, and you're more liberal-minded, it's no use to point out during a live shot that a certain city council ordinance in your eyes borders on civil rights violations. Remember, you're not there to give your own opinion, but to state frankly what is going on. As an open-minded individual, you may be the only reporter in town to get a bite with the local branch of the American Civil Liberties Union, instead of taking this story at face value.

YOU'RE ON YOUR OWN

One of the most difficult things you'll learn is, if you don't know something, not everyone is willing to help you find the answer. Find a mentor in the newsroom, if you can. Many times, you'll be on your own in figuring out what to do. That's why thinking on your feet is so important. If others at your station aren't very helpful, ask other friends in other markets for some of their tips and advice. And, watch big-market or network news; emulate reporters you like, or see how those stories were shot. See how those newscasts were produced. Much of your learning will be the on-the-job as-you-go-along type. Don't be discouraged. This makes for an exciting career, with every day bringing something different. However, it leaves a lot of room for error, because you'll literally be learning something new every day, whether it's building codes, criminal trials, sporting events, city budgets, or historical anniversaries. Think of yourself as the true Renaissance Person, knowing a little bit about a lot of things.

AVOIDING COMMON MISTAKES

Face it, you'll make a lot of mistakes along the way. Mistakes can be good, if you learn from them. However, there are some mistakes that you just can't make. And here's how to avoid them.

Make sure your scripts are read by at least one other seasoned individual in the newsroom. This is especially important when you're doing a story on crime, or government. We'll show you later on just why this is so imperative. If you're in a pressure situation, everyone is busy, and no one is available for help, you need to go with your instincts. You can call and ask someone at city council, for instance, if you're doing a city council story. Or call an attorney on the case, or

"My best advice to anyone starting out is the same advice that helped me. *Use* your *internship* to the maximum. Don't just sit there on the assignment desk answering phones and passing out newspapers. Get involved, beg different department heads to give you challenges and opportunities. When it comes time to hire someone, those qualities are always remembered. Plus, even if you don't get a job there, the experience will always stay with you."

Juan Hernandez, reporter

another trusted legal person, to make sure what you are saying is correct. This is not something to take lightly. Lawsuits are filed and careers ruined when facts aren't checked, or reporters aren't sure of the laws. To keep yourself from making these kinds of "fatal errors," as we call them, listen up and observe. Watch how stories are done and written by others, *before* you are put in a certain situation. We'll give you some legal tips and information in chapter 10.

A case in point: A brand-new reporter was sent to cover the local city council meeting (a beat that had lovingly been handed to her as the new kid on the block). There was another reporter there who had started work about the same time for a competing station. The council voted on an ordinance. Since the reporter was also the photographer, and was adjusting the camera, she didn't hear what the vote was, either yes or no. The fellow reporter told her that the proposal had passed. Not wanting to trust a competitor, she asked a council member after the meeting. He explained that the ordinance had indeed passed—a second reading, *but* that it was up for a third reading the next week. The ordinance was not a law yet . . . it still had to pass another reading. The council member said this was typical of just about every ordinance making its way through the system. She got the story right, and the competitor, who didn't wait until the end of the meeting, ended up misreporting that the ordinance had passed into law. Oops!

In a small station, and oftentimes in a big station, there is no one there to check your facts. Make a point to observe, and to ask, before you're put into a situation. One beginning reporter learned that the easy way. The competitor learned the hard way.

Even if you're an assignment editor or a producer, make it your job to know the status of these things. Even if the reporter had come back to the station with the incorrect idea in mind, this situation could have been avoided if the desk or the producer had known the status of the city council reading, and by knowing how the city council works. Don't just leave it up to the reporter at the scene; the assignment editor is the newsroom support system, the go-to person for information in the newsroom. In a small market, though, there is no desk or producer. The difference is, in a small town, in a small market, you can make these kinds of mistakes and continue on. If your first job is in a major market as a desk person, or a producer's assistant, the stakes are higher. Don't always rely on the reporter knowing this information, either. Many times, a reporter doesn't have a specific beat and is covering that particular story or beat for the first time. Check facts, talk to people, avoid mistakes, and impress your managers.

Still want to work in TV news after knowing "the scoop"? Read on.

There is no job training, no first-day orientation, or on-the-job seminar in TV news. Even the smallest markets will expect you to know what to do. So, find a mentor or a friend, *fast!*

2

YOU'VE GOT THE JOB,
WHAT DO YOU DO NOW?

You've edited and re-edited countless resumé tapes. Written and rewritten resumés and cover letters. Hey, the clerk at the local copy shop knows you by name. You've logged endless hours on your phone and even more in your car. And, finally, it's all paid off. You have your first, real TV job. Congratulations. Now what? Aside from packing up and moving out, here's some prep work you'll want to spend time on now, before you report for your first day of work.

KNOW YOUR NEW STATION'S BUSINESS

Who's the Boss?

Most U.S. television stations are part of media conglomerates, corporations, or networks. Few are locally owned and operated. If your station is part of a "chain," find out how many more stations make up the other links. Do a little research. Find out who'll be signing your

> "I practically begged the news director for the job. I ran teleprompter, ripped scripts, gathered chyron information, went out on stories as a reporter. I did anything I could to get experience."
>
> Erin Crowley, producer

checks. Sometimes it's not so easy. If you work for an O-and-O (owned and operated), you'll likely be part of an even bigger conglomerate, especially with the 2003 relaxing of FCC regulations. ABC is owned by a media conglomerate called Capital Cities, which is in turn owned by Disney. ESPN is also under this umbrella. General Electric owns NBC. Westinghouse owns CBS. Tribune owns more than a dozen stations nationwide, as does Gannett. It's likely that you'll end up working for one or more of these companies a few different times in your career. Remember that if you plan to burn bridges.

Where Do They Stand?

This one's simple. Television news is all about ratings. Is your station number one, two, three, four, or even five in the market? Find out. You can ask people at your station. Usually, it's pretty evident who the front-runner is. There are two types of front-runners, though; those who have been number one for so long, they take it for granted and are getting lazy; and then there's the fiercely competitive front-runner, who's aggressively trying to stay number one in the ratings.

Sample Newscasts

Request or record your own copies of the station's newscasts. Watch them. See how they do what they do. Pay attention to the presentation, the stories, the writing, the delivery, live shots, and graphics. These are important elements that will help you gauge how you can best fit in. But don't stop there. Look for ways you can put your own stamp on the established product.

Most newscasts and newsrooms are like salsas. Mild, medium, and hot. The mild ones stick to gathering the news with little flash or fanfare. The medium ones get the job done with a bit more creativity. They hit a hot story every once in a while. But the hot ones have it all. They seem to be everywhere. They know the news before it happens. And they bring it to their viewers in a timely, informative, and memorable way. Organization and experience are the key here.

Watch all the newscasts your station has to offer, if this applies. Usually an early newscast (typically 4 or 5 P.M., depending on your time zone) is an hour long and a lot lighter in its approach. Most start off with a news hit, then go on to lighter fare, like entertainment, cooking, or other similar types of segments. The 5 P.M. and the 10 P.M. (or 6 and 11 P.M. in other time zones) are usually the signature newscasts. Pay attention to these. Some stations do a "family-oriented" evening newscast, and then do more hard-hitting casts for the nighttime. Find out how your station stacks up, and what kinds of stories they do at different times. Also, is there an investigative unit that you've seen? These usually signal stations that are trying hard to either stay at number one or aggressively get there. This can also be a sign of a greater commitment to news than other stations.

Also, is "live" an integral factor in your station's newscasts? If it is, start practicing *now*. Think of a story in your head, or one you've heard recently. Pretend you're the reporter out on a live shot and stand in front of a mirror and jump right in. If you have a camcorder, tape yourself. How does it look? What can you do to improve things? How many times did you say "um, "like," or "uh"? Usually, live shots are best when they are concise. The best way to do this is to think of three important points, 1, 2, 3. List them off briefly. No one wants to see a reporter ramble on about unimportant information, or one who keeps repeating things. It's not easy, but you'll get the hang of it. If you're a producer or assignment editor, look to see what the station focuses on for live shots. This will give you a clue as to what that particular station deems important.

By watching the work before you go to work, you can have a better idea of how to craft your craft.

Take the Market Pulse

Compare your station with its competition. Assignment editors, pay attention to the types of stories you see. What's leading each station's newscast? Breaking news? Crime? Politics? Are they mainly stories you saw in the newspaper this morning, or are they hustled up? What you see is what you'll be expected to find and continue bringing to the table each day.

Producers, your focus should be on how the shows look, sound, and flow. The anchors on one station may whip through half a dozen stories before the other stations move past their lead. Check out the pace, use of graphics, and live shots. That in turn will give you a clue as to the writing style that will be expected of you. As we said, most stations are hot, mild, or somewhere in between.

Reporters, ask yourselves one question. Who in town gets and tells the best stories? What is the style of reporting like at your station? Do you see other reporters in the market that do a better job? Go for it! Do reporters tell the stories objectively or do they interject themselves in them? Do they use standups to forward the story along, or just to see themselves on TV? These are all things to look out for and observe.

Photographers, keep your eyes peeled to see if the other shooters in the market shoot to tell a story or simply shoot to fill the screen. Does your station use mainly VOs and VO/SOTs (voiceovers and voiceovers/sound on tape) or packages? That will determine how you shoot. Are most things handheld or tripod (you can tell it's handheld if there's a little "jiggle" in the shot)? Some stations have been known to hand down an edict that everything is handheld. A photographer with a bad back may not be so excited about that! How do the pictures tell the story? Are photographers shooting to communicate, or just filling airtime? A good photographer makes all the difference.

GET A JUMP-START

Regardless of your job in the newsroom, do three things before your first day on the job. Compile a basic list of contacts including police, fire, and city leaders. Look them up in the phone book; note their names when you see a bite from them on the air. That way, when you're asked to call so-and-so, you'll know who they are. Pay a visit to the local congressperson's office or give them a call. Ask them what the important issues are among their constituency. What drives the local economy? Who are the main players?

Have a partial Rolodex already started by the time you walk in the door on your first day.

Second, make yourself a "local" in the town you're working in,

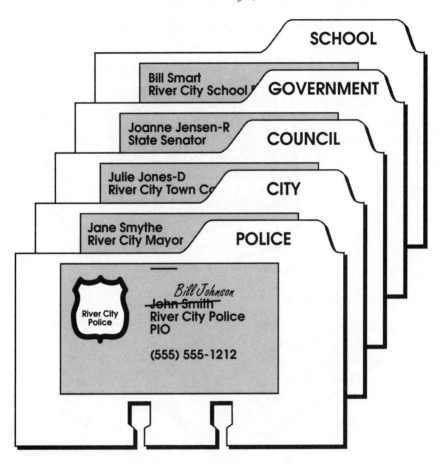

at least temporarily. *Learn the pronunciation* of places in your area. Can you say this? Natchitoches, Marc Racicot, Buena Vista? Answers: nak-o-dish, Mark Ros-coe, Beu-na vis-ta. Nothing turns off viewers to a new talent more than mispronouncing names and places that all the "locals" know. If you aren't sure of a word in a script, ask someone. Also, know where things are geographically. A weekend anchor recently asked a live reporter how far away a certain town was in relation to his own town. Anyone watching, except for the very newest viewers, could tell this anchor had no idea what he was talking about. Check these things out on a map, first. Hey, Internet maps are just a click away. And, make sure you find out what things are called locally,

Newsroom Operating Systems

too. For example, the Tri-County area. What does that mean? Don't mix it up and call it the Three-County area. It sounds simple, but many people make this basic but credibility-reducing mistake.

Same goes for words you may be unfamiliar with. An anchor in a small town once pronounced the word *botulism* just as it looks, like boat-al-ism, instead of the correct botch-you-lism. If you don't know, either ask, or in this case, you could look it up in the dictionary. Then write it out phonetically in the script for yourself, if you need to. Botch-you-lism. Chances are, if you can't pronounce the word, you probably don't even know what the story is about. And that's why you're there in the first place, to relay information.

And, third, if you have any time at all, practice on your newsroom computer. Deadlines have a way of sneaking up on you and the last thing you need is to be slowed down by the technology that's designed to speed you up.

THIS COULD HAPPEN

Believe it or not, you could very likely get your first job over the phone, sight unseen. If you're a reporter, all the news director may know of you is what's on your tape, your resumé, and how you handled a few phone conversations. You may be moving to an unknown small town without knowing a soul. How do you get ahead in this situation?

Our Advice

First, get a map. If it's a small town, where in the state is the town you're hired to work in? As we said, don't be afraid to use the Internet. Almost every town, regardless of size, has a website. It will usually list the movers and shakers, such as who's mayor, who's on the town council, and so on. It'll also generally have local news stories, what's going on, and what's important to the community. If you're moving to another state, do the same at the state level. Who's the governor? What drives the state's economy?

Call the newsroom. Talk to reporters, producers, assignment editors there, anyone. What's it like to work there? Don't encourage gossip; just ask what kind of stories they cover, how the newsroom works, and the like. Ask for that sample tape. Ask about the town, where to live, how much an apartment costs. In small markets, that small salary might not feel so bad when you find out that rent is fairly low, too. Call the newspaper, see if they'll send you a copy, or see if they have a website. This is a great way to see for yourself about apartments and availability, plus find out what's going on around town.

Follow these steps and you'll be one step ahead of the game when you walk in the door that first day.

Be a Boy Scout. Always be prepared.

3

YOUR FIRST DAY

The first day in a newsroom, no matter how big or small, can be overwhelming. The first thing you're likely to notice is the lack of order. This is no ordinary office. It's more like an ordinary office in fast-forward, constantly. Phones ringing, printers printing, scanners and TVs blaring, and people talking, laughing, and sometimes freaking out. Your first inclination may be to call for a time out. Or to back away and quietly sneak out the back door. But the reality is, if you want to work in television news, you have to take the leap. Jump right in. Sort of like getting in the swimming pool on that first sunny sum-

"I love my job because it is often unpredictable. I get a rush from breaking news . . . being the first to know about an event and having to digest the information quickly as I spontaneously let viewers know what I just learned. I enjoy the challenge of having to convey the information clearly without the proper preparation. If you are good at 'winging' it . . . this business is for you.

"I also meet so many interesting people and telling their stories is sometimes quite an honor. Preparing for a big interview is invigorating. I can't wait to ask the important questions and hear their response. But, not all stories have happy endings, so I get a daily dose of reality."

Debbie Denmon, anchor

mer day. You know the water is cold. You feel like you should go slowly, but finally you dive right in. Sure, it's a shock at first. You may even gasp for air, but eventually you adjust to the new environment and even start to enjoy it.

SETTLING IN

We can honestly say, in our experience in ten-plus newsrooms, that we've never had a first day when we could actually "settle in." And no one we've talked to has had that luxury either. More likely, you should plan to come in a day early. But on the off chance you do get the opportunity to get settled on your first official day, use it! Usually your first day will be spent "jumping in," instead of "settling in."

COME PREPARED

Dress the part. If you're a reporter, wear clothes suitable for air. And maybe bring a pair of jeans, and a polo-type shirt, along with comfortable shoes, and just keep them in your car. What if you're sent out to cover a forest fire, or flood, on your first day? You'd feel a little out of place in a suit and tie (plus, your favorite pair of shoes will get absolutely ruined.) Ladies, you don't want to be tramping around a

---

Newsroom Survival Kit

Change of clothes
Briefcase/knapsack/oversized purse
Pens
Notebooks
Maps of area for your car
Rolodex®
Makeup/hairspray
Universal earpiece (for reporters)
Pack a lunch and snacks

---

muddy flooded area in those suede high heels you bought just for the occasion. Bring a sturdy pair of tennis shoes. Men and women, bring makeup, hairbrushes, combs, and yes, hairspray. These things likely won't be provided, and if you're out in the field, you'll need your own anyway. Men, you don't want to be doing a live shot in a dark area at night, and have your forehead reflecting like a beacon. Wear colors you know you look good in. Avoid white and gray, you'll look washed out.

Producers and assignment editors, you can afford to be a little more comfortable wardrobe-wise, while still looking professional. If you actually interviewed at the station, take note of what news staff are wearing.

Bring a briefcase, a backpack, a knapsack . . . whatever . . . something to carry all of your stuff. Stock up on pens and notebooks. There isn't a newsroom on earth that has enough pens to go around. Invest in an organizer with a calendar. Bring your Rolodex that you compiled. You may feel like a nerd at first, but everyone is so busy, no one will even notice, and it won't take long for these tools to come in handy.

HIT THE GROUND RUNNING

How many times have you heard this one? It's true. In a television newsroom, you have no choice. It's literally sink or swim. There won't be anyone with the time to take you around for introductions and orientation. People will assume you automatically know what's going on, even in a small market. So, blaze your own trail, and take it upon yourself to meet everyone and learn how they fit in.

Now that that's out of the way, sit down and get acquainted with your computer. We can't stress this one enough. Practice, practice, practice. Offer to write a couple of VOs. Have someone give you a sample script. That way you can become familiar with script formatting and ask questions without facing a deadline pressure cooker.

Assignment Editors

Even if you never write a script at the station, you'll certainly be referring to them for information. Learn them, inside and out. People will call you with complaints . . . you'll be the one to look up last night's script and see what it said. Then you'll need to figure out who wrote

VO SAMPLE

I-47 AX
LAURA SINGLE
BOX/CAR AX
 	
TAKE VO
TAPE JOHNSON 14
*cg line2 I-47 AND MAPLE AVENUE/
THIS AFTERNOON
 	
SHOW AMBULANCE TAKING AWAY
VICTIM, TAPE G-72 3:14:27
	((LAURA))
	    A BIG ACCIDENT TIES UP TRAFFIC FOR
	HOURS ON EASTBOUND INTERSTATE 47
	RIGHT IN THE MIDDLE OF TOWN.
	((------------VO------------))
	    WITNESSES SAY THE DRIVER OF A
	PICK-UP SUDDENLY SWERVED INTO THE
	CONCRETE MEDIAN, SPUN AROUND,
	AND HIT SEVERAL OTHER VEHICLES.
	    IT HAPPENED AROUND THREE-THIRTY
	THIS AFTERNOON.
	    THE CHAIN REACTION WRECKED
	SEVENTEEN VEHICLES IN ALL.
	    A DOZEN PEOPLE WERE HURT. FIVE
	WERE TAKEN TO THE HOSPITAL. NO ONE
	WAS SERIOUSLY HURT.
	    THE DRIVER WHO POLICE SAY CAUSED
	THE ACCIDENT COULD FACE RECKLESS
	DRIVING CHARGES.

it and go back to the source. You'll need to know where to look on the script for all these pieces of information.

Producers

How long is each story? How will it fit into the newscast? What if you want to change or update a piece of information? Who's working on which story? You'll need to do all of these things with scripts.

Reporters

It's obvious why you need to know the system. And you can't learn it fast enough. A half-hour before news time isn't the time to be wondering how you deleted your entire story by accident.

Photographers / Editors

You may not think that knowing your way around the computer system is imperative, but it is. All the assignment files are in them, containing information on shoots, like where you're going, who you're talking to, what the story is about. You won't always be out with a reporter, so you'll need to have this information in hand. If the desk is busy, no one's going to want to take the time to print out this information for you. It's up to you.

And, when you go to edit a story, you've got to know the cues on the script. Who wrote the story, how many seconds of the car accident do you edit before you put up a picture of the victim? And where does the story fall in the show? First block, or after weather? You'll need to access a rundown on the computer for all that information. Like just about any company in existence today, a newsroom can't function without the computer.

LISTEN FIRST. ASK QUESTIONS LATER

Keep your ears open and remember these three letters: O-A-A. They are very important to recall when you're about to ask a question of anyone in a newsroom.

```
O-A-A

O-Observe
A-Absorb
A-Ask
```

- O—Observe. Watch what your co-workers are doing and how they do it.
- A—Absorb. Commit what you observe to memory. Then,
- A—Ask.

You stand a better chance of getting an answer and not a glare of disdain if you follow O-A-A. Put it this way: it's like being in a foreign country. If you just go up to someone and start talking in loud English, they most likely won't respond. But if you at least have a working knowledge of their language and you throw in the few words that you do know, people are much more willing to help.

Case in point: a news photographer. First job. Small market station. Back in the days of ¾-inch videotape. That's when the camera was connected, via a cable, to a huge tape deck that the photographer lugged around like a piece of carry-on baggage. The photog and reporter arrive at a story location. They unload the equipment. The photog sets up and starts to shoot video. That's when the reporter notices both the camera and the deck, but no connecting cable. The photographer failed to ask anyone *how* to properly operate the equipment *before* she went out on her first shoot. An embarrassing and completely avoidable situation, and one co-workers never forget. These are the stories that linger in newsrooms long after you're gone.

THIS COULD HAPPEN

Assignment Editors

The assignment manager takes a break for lunch. You're by yourself on the desk. No big deal . . . the scanners are quiet, you're entering in information for some story ideas you got from the newspaper, and waiting for follow-up calls. All your crews are out on stories or are on lunch break. Your boss, the managing editor, and the news director are in all-day budget meetings and have asked that they not be bugged unless it's something big.

All hell breaks loose on the scanner. You can hear different cops, out of breath, and one of them is yelling. Dispatch seems confused too, asking what happened. You turn up the scanner, hear someone yell "Officer down!" This could be big, but where is it happening? There are so many districts on the scanner, you can't even tell which police or sheriff's department to call. No one's around to ask for help. The phone rings, and someone wants some information on a story that aired last night. They're irritated, saying the station made a mistake. Meanwhile the scanner is still going nuts. What do you do?

PIO: Public Information Officer

The main contact for an organization, like police and fire departments, city and county governments, and the like. Many times the only person in the organization allowed to go on-camera or give "official" information.

Our Advice

First, get rid of the caller. Politely, of course. Tell him you're very busy but will look up the information and get back to him. Get his number and get off the phone. Start with the list of police and sheriff's districts. This may help, but if an officer down situation is really going on, dispatch isn't going to take time to help you right now. Like you, they've got their hands full, and they are dealing with a potentially life-threatening situation. Instead, call PIOs of all the surrounding districts. It's lunchtime, so you may have to page them instead. (See how important those contact phone numbers are? You can't afford to be wasting time looking for them when you should be dispatching a photographer. If you have a cell phone, you can store those important numbers in your phone book and look them up really fast.)

Next, while you wait to hear back and continue monitoring the scanner, call your crews. Photographers have scanners in their cars, and sometimes carry them. Ask if they're hearing what you are. Many even know the scanner channel frequencies by heart and can tell at a glance just which district the call is coming from. Continue listening for any clue as to the location of the scene, like a street name, then send a crew ASAP. The important thing here is to keep your head and get as much information as you can as soon as you can.

Photographers

You're new on the job and have shot a few packages, and several VOs and VO/SOTs. So you feel fairly comfortable on the equipment, although you know it will take some time to get up to the speed you'll need for really breaking situations. You're eating your lunch in the newsroom when you hear about a shooting at a local high school. You're geared up to go out to the scene, but what do you do once you get there? The assignment editor is frantic to get you out the door but isn't giving you any direction beyond that. What do you do?

Our Advice

Head to the scene. That's why it's so important to know your way around town. This isn't the time to ask anyone for directions. Okay, you're there, but it's chaos and no one seems to know where the gunman is, who the gunman is, or if anyone is seriously hurt. At this point, police have probably already set up a "staging area" for media. This is still a dangerous situation. Kids are running out of the school. You can ask what's going on, but keep in mind that rumors are rife at this point, and you may miss something else, like cops leading the gunman out of the building in handcuffs. You probably want to concentrate on that right now, and grab some student interviews later. Stay in constant contact with the station and with cops or sheriffs. They are your connection to information. Keep listening to the scanner, too. And finally, when things start to shake out or calm down a little, let the station know what you have. Producers and assignment editors are trying to organize all the information, and this will help immensely.

This is a situation where you've got to play things by ear. But being prepared for the unexpected is helping you out. You've white-balanced, you have those extra tapes and batteries that have come in handy. You got that shot of the student being led away in handcuffs because you had that extra battery. You're like the fireman, waiting and waiting and waiting, and when the worst comes, you're ready to handle it.

Reporters / Producers

It's your first day. Soon after you walk in the door, shake a few hands, and make the rounds, the assignment editor sends you off to the city council meeting. Your assignment: sit in and listen. Sounds easy enough. The producer just needs information on a controversial issue for a VO. You dutifully oblige. Once there, you listen as council members pass legislation on the sticky issue. But none of the other reporters or photographers in the room seem to realize what just happened. Could this be a scoop? What do you do? Are you not understanding what's going on? How do you find out if your hunch is right?

Our Advice

Start by calling the station. The assignment editor, anchors, and reporters likely know bits and pieces of the history of the issue. Listen to what they have to say. Tell them what you saw and heard. Then hang up and go find the council clerk. Ask what happened and what it means. If you have a hunch you're on to something, be discreet about it. It could be you just landed an exclusive on your first day. And a lot of respect from your co-workers.

How else can you earn respect among your peers? Notice we said "earn." It's a key word. No matter what school or big market you came from, you're only as good as your last story or newscast. Hold it together. It's always admirable to keep your head under pressure. And others will be watching how you handle yourself. If you lose it, it'll take a long time for people to forget. If you're a reporter and you freak out, you may be passed over when those exciting spot news stories come along, and instead be sent to city council. If you're a producer, or producer assistant, you may end up as a writer or on the overnight shift. That's why it's so important to know what to do ahead of time in any situation.

Pitch In

This point is so important that we'll go back to it again and again. If you're just getting off your assignment desk shift, and you hear breaking news over the scanner, don't walk away. Make calls. Write a story and give the producer time to deal with this changing situation. It'll also give you additional experience that you just can't buy.

Here's a case in point:

It's Sunday night, ten minutes after the news is over. The producer, assistant producer, and photographer are the only ones left at the station. The photographer is just walking out the door. The scanner goes nuts. It's apparently a car accident, a bad one on a dangerous two-lane road. Sounds like multiple victims. The producer and her assistant ask the photographer to get video of the accident. He argues, saying since the station only has one newscast at night, no one is going to care about a car accident twenty-four hours from now. It'll be old news by then. The producers stand firm. The photographer asks that the producers use the photographer on call, since it's technically after the newscast. That won't be fast enough, and besides this photographer is ready to head out the door, geared up. The photographer ends up going, although he doesn't want to, out to what all three think is a "typical" car accident that will end up being a VO tomorrow, or maybe not even run at all.

Turns out the accident was caused by a drunk driver who crossed the line, and among the victims is a little girl. The drunk is in bad shape and is going to be airlifted to the hospital. The chopper takes off, then hits power lines and crashes. All on board are killed. Guess who was first at the scene, who got video just seconds before the crash, with the medical staff inside the chopper working to save the driver's life? Every station in town was doing cut-ins at midnight, updating people on what happened. It was the biggest news story in town for a long time. Who had video? If the producers had just decided to ignore the scanner too, the Big Story would have passed them by.

Sure, news staff worked until 3 A.M., but sometimes that's what it takes. News doesn't always happen during working hours.

And, it can be *dangerous*. Don't think you won't get shot, punched,

"This business can sometimes be dangerous. Once I was doing a live report in front of the King county courthouse in Seattle and was attacked. The dramatic event played out on live television. Remember that hiding behind the camera and notebook won't stop a bullet or a punch."

Dan Lothian, network reporter

or assaulted just because you're "in the media." There are numerous stories about journalists getting roughed up, or barely escaping a dangerous situation. Think about it. You're sent to cover a riot, with a lot of drunk college kids still running around, setting fires, throwing rocks and bottles, and so on. You're sent to cover a sniper who's still on the loose. Don't go rushing into a dark alley without checking with the police first. You're sent on a blazing wildfire. It's night, small town, black as can be. Suddenly the wind changes direction, and the wildfire is all around you. No wonder the firefighters didn't want you to drive this way, even though you ended up talking your way through the lines. No story is worth jeopardizing your safety or the safety of others who may have to go in to rescue you.

> **Rely on your instincts. The unexpected is bound to happen.**

4

PUTTING IT ALL TOGETHER: CAST AND CREW

WHO'S WHO IN THE NEWSROOM

Now that you work in a newsroom, how does everyone fit together and what's expected of each position, including yours? Sure, you read your job description, but those are only general guidelines. In reality, you're expected implicitly to do a lot more, to give a lot more, than what's written in the Human Resources Handbook. And, what better way to work your way up the ladder or into a larger market?

We've listed the main positions that you'll find in any newsroom. Some may have more, and more specific, jobs, and most, especially small newsrooms, will have fewer jobs. In those cases, you'll be expected to wear many hats.

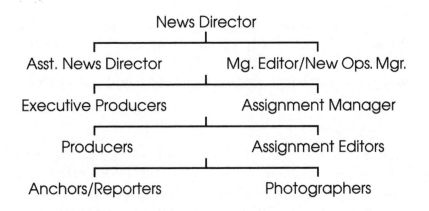

The graphic on page 29 gives a rough indication of how a newsroom may be structured. While it is accurate about job responsibilities, it can be deceiving. Why are reporters and anchors on the "bottom"? Technically, they take direction from the producer, who takes direction from the executive producer, who is responsible to the news director. Many anchors, though, share in the day-to-day decision-making process, as a managing editor or executive producer would. However, the actual person responsible for an on-air mistake would be the producer. Anchors may help make decisions about story treatment (the angle of the story), or whether to do a story at all, but the producer would have to answer to the news director in cases of factual errors and the like.

Behind-the-scenes people bear this in mind: You may not be fond of some of the talent you work with. They may not be fond of you. But remember, they are the representatives of the entire news station to the public. It bears a great responsibility. If they flub up, the station looks bad. If you flub up, the people around you know you did it, and the talent still looks bad. In the case of power struggles, 99 times out of 100, the talent will win. If the situation escalates, the producer will be the one sent packing, not the talent. Kind of like a football team. Generally, the coach will be asked to leave instead of the star quarterback. Yes, it's a measure of security for that person; however, they have that increased pressure to always perform well, every time.

MANAGEMENT

We'll start with the most important positions in the newsroom, at least the ones you'll want to make a good showing to, to keep your job.

Managers come in all shapes and sizes, and generally, the number of managers is directly related to the size of the market and station.

Large Market

Large markets will have a general manager, the head honcho at the station. They will ultimately have a say in your future at the station. Remember, most GMs come from a sales background, so money is the bottom line, and whether you're a good journalist will be somewhere down the line in importance. Also, in today's world of conglomerates, GMs oftentimes answer to some other corporate head, who's watching the station's bottom line, many times from a distant headquarters in another city.

The news director will answer to the GM. In large markets, the ND's time is mostly taken up with budget meetings, news promotions, and administrative tasks. However, the ND will often have the final say on hirings, firings, and layoffs.

The assistant news director, or in some cases, the managing editor, is the next in line, and generally oversees the day-to-day operations in the newsroom. That means being involved in the news assignment meetings, helping make decisions on news content, and being a legal advisor, when those types of questions arise that he or she can handle. The assistant news director/managing editor is also generally the most hands-on in hiring newsroom personnel, looking at tapes and resumés. This will most likely be your point of contact for a position in a large market station. And sometimes there may be more than one, working in tandem, someone who's in control during the day, the other at night.

Smaller market stations will most likely have a variation of these managers. The smaller the market is, the more hands-on the news director is, and he or she will wear most of these management hats. Sometimes the news director is also the main anchor, as well as the producer and the nightside assignment editor.

THE NEWSROOM AND YOU

Now that we have management out of the way, let's get down to the positions you'd most likely be applying for. Warning! A job description in television news is just that, a job description. It's the beginning, not the end of what will be expected of you. We've broken it down this way: A responsibility breakdown, and the reality.

Assignment Editor: Responsibilities

The assignment editor is one of the most pivotal, and one of the most underrated positions in the newsroom. A job description will mention that this person must:

- Determine which stories to cover
- Assign news crews to cover them
- Answer phones
- Collect mail and faxes, and sort through them
- File appropriate press releases under the date that the event will take place
- Listen for spot news over the scanner.

Reality

That sounds like a lot, but it's not even the half of it. Overall, the assignment editor must have excellent news judgment and must be able to make decisions at the drop of a hat. You really must be a self-starter for this job. A thick skin helps, too.

Basically, you are the gatekeeper for the newsroom. Answering every phone call that comes to the newsroom means everything from people confirming press releases, calls from "tipsters," calls from viewers, many of whom are disgruntled for some reason or another, people requesting tapes of stories they saw on the news, people calling about programming other than news, people calling about commercials they see on your air (yes, it's true!), and callbacks from people reporters have contacted and need to talk to.

At the same time, you need to:

- Monitor the news wires (these are on the computer and are generally very easy to pull up)
- Generate news stories on your own
- Run the assignment meetings with the news staff
- Make calls on stories you saw on the wires, in press releases, in the papers, heard over the scanner, or saw on competing news stations
- Keep track of court hearings and court dates, and file the correct paperwork to ask the court if cameras will be allowed in
- Know where every news employee is at any given time
- Take calls from news crews in the field, and make calls for them, to pass along information when they need it
- Make spot news decisions.

SCENARIO

A news crew is on the way to a hastily called press conference regarding a series of rapes on a local college campus. Authorities won't tell you, but you suspect they have caught a serial rapist who has been inciting fear among college women. Bottom line: you can't miss this story. Meanwhile, you hear over the scanner that there's a high-speed chase going on through a very busy section of town. Car chases have been a big story recently, because a prominent person was hit and killed during an incident last week. Your dilemma: the car chase is near your news crew and not near the station. It could end quickly. Do you divert your news crew on the way to the press conference, hoping they'll luck out and catch the car chase on tape, and risk missing the press conference, or do you send a photographer who's at the station, who may miss the car chase? Remember, the car chase may turn out to be nothing, but you don't want to risk the chance that some other innocent person could be hurt, and therefore miss another big story. What do you do?

See where the thick skin comes in? Folks are always going to be questioning your judgment—usually people who weren't around at the time. And you won't always make the right decisions, because the situation can change rapidly. Tough decisions. And one thing is sure. No one is going to thank you if you make the right choices, but you'll sure hear about it if you make the wrong ones!

> "The biggest challenge is learning you can't please everyone and accepting that you will never be perfect. Viewers can be harsh when you are anchoring so thick skin is a must and as far (as) reporting you are only as good as your last story."
> Debbie Denmon, anchor

The upside: the assignment editor has a lot of say in shaping each day's news programs, and that's exciting. And, you're the one in the driver's seat when you get an exclusive story. Plus, it's just an exciting job. . . . you'll never be watching the clock, counting the minutes until the day is over. Time flies by. And like every other position in the newsroom, the most attractive of qualities about a news job is you do something different every day, and learn something new every day.

Producer: Responsibilities

- Determines story placement in the newscast (called "stacking")
- Determines story treatment (live shot, VO, VO/SOT, package—we talk about these formats below)
- Writes teases
- Determines graphics, over-the-shoulder boxes, and cutlines for them (the catch phrases written underneath the boxes)

Two essential characteristics of a news producer are an ability to handle pressure, and organizational skills. A good producer will make sure every last detail is taken care of in a newscast, even under the utmost pressure. It's not easy, and that's why producers are one of the most sought-after employees in TV news.

Reality

Producers have a lot of control over the news shows and can really take a lot of pride in that. Optimally, the producer should:

- Know the content of each story, and "stack" the newscast so each story flows into the next. (This includes amending the tags and lead-ins of stories to help with flow, while not changing the content or reporter's meaning, a sure balancing act.)
- Write stories not written by other reporters, anchors, or assistants in the newsroom.
- Read all the stories, leads, tosses to live shots, and so on, to make sure everything makes sense.
- Rewrite some of these items, and constantly make changes.
- Continually change show lineup as the day progresses, spot news comes up, or other stories don't pan out.
- Monitor that everything is going smoothly, that stories are being edited, that scripts are in order, that news feeds from the satellite are being taken by the engineers, and generally, that the show will be ready when the time comes.

- Keep in touch with field crews to ensure they are on the right track, too, and will be ready in time for air.
- Check with engineering to make sure live shots will be there when they are needed.
- Ensure fonts are spelled correctly.
- Keep in touch with the desk who is monitoring spot news, or monitor the scanner yourself, if there is no night desk.
- Line produce the show. This means sitting in the broadcast booth, talking into the anchors' earpieces or IFBs during the show, and making spot decisions to add or drop stories to have the show come out exactly on time, sometimes to the second.

"The trick is, as a producer anyway, trying to get people to carry out your vision of the newscast, and doing it in a way that doesn't detract from what they bring to their own job."
Erin Crowley, producer

Reporters: Responsibilities

A large part of a reporter's job is spent away from the station, so this is a job that requires a lot of thinking on the go.

- Go out on stories, and put together what's called a news package. That is a story with reporter voiceover, soundbites, and a reporter standup. Many times the reporter will do a "wraparound" live shot or "on-set piece." A wraparound live is when the anchors "toss" to the reporter, the reporter "tosses" to the package, comes back out of the package, and "tosses" back to the anchors at the station. An on-set piece is basically the same thing, except the reporter sits on the news set with the anchors.

Reality

As a reporter, you will:

- Either receive a story assignment at the beginning of your shift, or come up with a story during the assignment meeting.

- Make calls and set up interviews yourself.
- Write other stories for the newscast, or make calls on other stories running in the newscast.
- Make contacts in many different areas: police, fire, hospitals, city council, and so on.
- Be asked, depending on market size, to edit your own stories and other stories, and you may be asked to assist in setting up live shots.
- Need to know a lot about a lot of different subjects. One day you may do a story on chemicals used during the Vietnam conflict, and the next, a story on a homeowner's lawsuit against a developer.
- Read the newspaper and be aware of what the stories are, just in case you're assigned to do something out of the paper.
- Bring your own stories to the table. These can come from other stories you did that generated ideas, or from talking to people out in the field. Some of these stories can come from your story file. We'll talk more about that in the next chapter.
- Follow up on stories you did earlier. Don't make this just the assignment editor's job. Do it yourself. It's called "owning" the story.

Photographer: Responsibilities

- Shoot video for newscast, assigned by assignment desk or producer.
- Edit stories as needed.

Reality

- Run from story to story, oftentimes working by yourself.
- Become your own reporter. You'll often need to ask questions and pick up SOTs on your own.
- "Write" news stories visually. It's your job not just to shoot, but to tell stories with pictures.
- Be on-call as necessary. That means being ready twenty-four hours a day to go when you're called, even if it's 4 A.M. and a major blizzard is brewing.

- Edit not only the stories you shoot, but many times other things for the newscast.
- Set up live shots, possibly even run a microwave truck, after you've shot and edited a news package.
- Stand out in any weather for news conferences, at courthouses, people's homes, and so on.
- Since you are around the scanners all day, you'll likely be the one to sit at the assignment desk when everyone's at lunch, or even at night, when some stations don't staff a desk. Guess who's responsible for spot news?
- Put yourself in dangerous, potentially deadly situations at times. You'll be the one shooting video of the crazed guy with a gun holed up in a home, or the school shooting when nobody knows just exactly where the gunman is; you'll be the one going into fires, floods, and tornadoes. For some photographers, this is the reason why they love this job.

NOT FOR THE FAINT OF HEART

No matter which job you hold in the newsroom, you will most likely see things you would rather not. Field crews see them firsthand, others on the unedited videotape.

This is a word of caution: get ready to see things that will disturb you. Some people just aren't prepared. You may see horrific auto accidents, oftentimes before bodies are removed. You may see a shooting victim's brains on the sidewalk. Sometimes victims are children. Sometimes you'll witness the first reactions that people have upon learning of the death of a loved one. It's times like these when you realize that you're not just covering stories, you're covering people and *their* stories. Be prepared.

> "I try to go beyond the facts, beyond good sound, to get great sound. And to do that I have to build up trust in my subjects, to get to know them and find out their character."
>
> Eric Kehe, photographer

NOT JUST THE NEWS

Of course, the newsroom isn't the only department in the station, and many of the other departments will be integral to the way you work.

Production Department

The production department is one you'll work closely with. The director, technical director, audio engineer, studio camera people, and the graphics person are usually in the production department. They are the folks that take care of things technically during the newscast. They ensure the studio camera is set up for over-the-shoulder shots with the anchors (which are a little to one side to make room for the box), they switch to the appropriate anchor who is reading, make sure the teleprompter has the proper script loaded, that the appropriate boxes and names come up during the right story, that the right mics are potted up and down, that live shots are technically working and available when needed, and so on.

Production photographers often shoot commercials and station promotions.

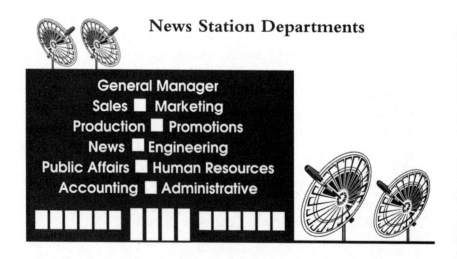

News Station Departments

General Manager
Sales ■ Marketing
Production ■ Promotions
News ■ Engineering
Public Affairs ■ Human Resources
Accounting ■ Administrative

Engineering Department

You'll also work closely with the engineering department. Engineers technically keep the station on the air, make sure the newscast is running smoothly, and tune in live shots and satellite lives. They'll also take special feeds for you, if they are needed. (A special feed is something that is sent via satellite, maybe some video from a sister station on breaking news, etc.)

Promotions Department

The promotions department does just that: promotions. They write promotional spots for the news department and for station programming. These folks also come up with station promotions, maybe working with the local zoo to sponsor a News5 Zoo Day, for example. As a news person, especially an on-air talent, you'll be asked to participate (i.e., "The benefit was hosted by News5's own Jessica Smith"). Promotions can often be associated with sales.

Sales Department

The sales department is the station cash register; that is, it makes the money. These people are the ones who sell airtime. There are local sales managers and staff, and national sales managers and staff. Above them all is the general sales manager.

PUBLIC AFFAIRS DEPARTMENT

These folks take care of community-oriented projects and air public service announcements, or PSAs. An example of this is an anti-drug campaign. All stations are required to air a certain number of PSAs by law. Public Affairs is also in place to help the station's "image," that is, it promotes all of the good things the station does in the community.

WRAP-UP

You might wonder just why you would need to know what everyone else's job is. It's one of the most powerful things you can know. Once you realize what everyone else is supposed to be doing, you can gauge what your role is. It helps you work as part of a team and understand just what's going on. This is especially important during times of spot news, when everything needs to be in place, because things are moving so quickly. Even on a daily basis, no newscast can make air without a team effort. Every position relies on every other position to make it all work.

You'll never know when you'll be called upon (or will just need to volunteer) to help out. How can you jump in and run the assignment desk if you don't know what those people do all day? We can't stress enough the team effort. So many news people focus only on what they are doing all day, that they forget that others are working just as hard, with just as much frustration and pressure, too. No one has an "easy" job!

We also wanted to show you that some of the most exciting roles in television news are not necessarily in front of the camera. Every job is indeed important, glamorous in its own way, and definitely interesting.

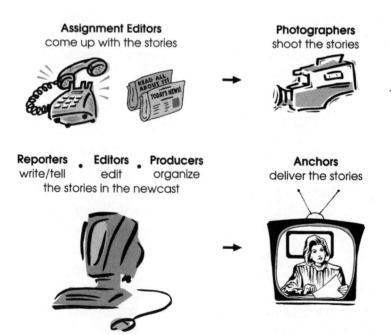

Assignment Editors
come up with the stories

Photographers
shoot the stories

Reporters · **Editors** · **Producers**
write/tell   edit   organize
the stories in the newcast

Anchors
deliver the stories

Here's a situation that really happened. A news anchor interested in animal rights had set up a story on an animal preserve, the type where wild animals are kept. The story was set up for a holiday, so that the station would have a good, solid story on a typically slow news day.

A reporter was assigned the story, really a no-brainer. During her stand-up, she put her hand too close to a bear's cage, and was bitten. She was rushed to the hospital and was subsequently okay, even though she lost the tip of her finger. At first she told the newsroom that she didn't want that portion of the story told, she was somewhat embarrassed. But as the day wore on, and she had time to think about it, she determined that she wanted the injury included in the story. She felt the owners of the preserve shouldn't continue to allow people close access to the cages. A photographer who had done a similar story there before said he had heard of others being bitten. When the anchors and the producer got in that afternoon, a squall was definitely brewing. The anchor who had set up the story was reluctant to mention the bite, feeling the reporter should have known better. The point of the story was to show viewers the plight of these animals, that the preserve owners were doing a service to these animals, and that they needed funds to help keep the place going. The reporter (calling in from home) was just as vehement about mentioning what had happened and possibly changing the focus of the story to the dangers of the place. The producer felt that it was part of the story, it had happened, and should at least be mentioned, but not made the focal point of the story. Others in the newsroom had strong views either way. The issue was debated for hours, with the reporter and management calling in their views on the phone.

In the end, the straight story on the preserve was run, but the tag mentioned that the reporter had been bitten, and reminded anyone who visited the preserve that wild animals are wild and will act accordingly.

The story could have gone many different directions, but everyone in the newsroom got involved, regardless of their position.

Holistic Approach: In television news, you are more than the sum total of your job description.

5

NEWSROOM SURVIVAL GUIDE

We said it before, but we'll say it again, your job description and what you really do may be vastly different. Survival in a newsroom depends on it. For instance, if you're a reporter and have an Emmy Award–winning story, the story won't matter if your editor either doesn't have time to edit it or goes home with the stomach flu. Learn how to edit; it may not be the best job in the world, but it will be done, and then your story will hit air. If you're an assignment editor it might be a good idea to be able to write for the newscast. If you're a producer be ready to jump in and report. Bottom line, be as prepared as possible for anything. Smaller market stations are often the places where a flexible, multitalented person can stand out. And, they are the best places to learn. So, do it. The more you know, the better and more valuable you'll be.

WORKING FAIR

As you settle into your job, pay close attention to what and how much your co-workers are doing on a daily basis. By the very nature of their jobs, assignment editors could easily run a reporter and photographer into the ground sending them from shoot to shoot. A producer could overload a photographer/editor with too many stories to edit for the show. Or a reporter can put pressure on everyone by being disorganized and not getting his or her share done in time. Re-

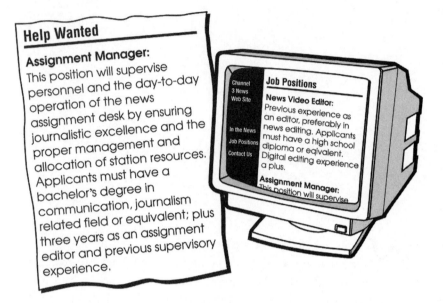

Help Wanted

Assignment Manager:
This position will supervise personnel and the day-to-day operation of the news assignment desk by ensuring journalistic excellence and the proper management and allocation of station resources. Applicants must have a bachelor's degree in communication, journalism related field or equivalent; plus three years as an assignment editor and previous supervisory experience.

Channel 3 News Web Site
In the News
Job Positions
Contact Us

Job Positions

News Video Editor:
Previous experience as an editor, preferably in news editing. Applicants must have a high school diploma or eqivalent. Digital editing experience a plus.

Assignment Manager:
This position will supervise

member, your writing the story is just part of the process. It still needs to be edited, and maybe microwaved back to the station if you're on a live shot. Put yourself in your co-workers' shoes and chances are better they won't be tempted to throw them at you.

Always keep tabs on the time. Can that coffee break wait until you've finished writing the story or edited that piece? Most news

folks learn to eat on the go, anyway. Assignment editors, don't leave the station until all your daily files are updated. A producer won't be happy if you left without putting down the address of the staging area for a forest fire that broke out just before your shift was over. Neither will the field crew who will lose valuable time driving around the woods, trying to determine just where the press is supposed to meet with the forest service. Thinking ahead is key here. Sure, you'll probably spend a lot of extra time at the station, but that's what this career is all about.

> "I knew it was going to be very low-paying, long hours and high stress. I was fortunate to know people in the business who did not put rose-colored glasses on me."
> Hayley Herst, assignment manager

If you don't follow these simple suggestions, life in a newsroom can become very hard, very fast. Reporters, you'll be sent on the most boring stories. Your stories won't have that extra flair that an editor's creative edge can give. And oh, your stand-up didn't look so great either, but the photographer didn't bother telling you your lipstick was on your tooth. Assignment editors, field crews will stop calling in and telling you where they are and what they're doing. Then, when the boss wants to know what's going on, guess who doesn't have that important information? Producers, there's no end to the misery that will

> "A skill that can't be taught and that comes with experience only is learning how to deal with people, no matter the job. There are so many different personalities in a newsroom, so many people with different agendas, so many egos. Often it's difficult to get the job done because some people fight what you're trying to do or because they are constant complainers."
> Erin Crowley, producer

be yours if you don't treat others with respect—such as, stories won't make it to air, or they will come in at the last possible moment, or that satellite feed you really needed wasn't tuned to the proper coordinates. See what we mean? And yes, not everyone will be professional and treat you with respect. But make it your motto to be as professional as you can at all times, even under great stress. You'll go far.

FRIENDS IN ALL THE RIGHT PLACES

Ever heard the phrase, *don't burn your bridges?* It's especially important to remember those four words when you work in a newsroom. Make friends with the right people and your job will be measurably easier. Reporters, don't underestimate the power of the desk or the camera. Assignment editors and photographers can make all the difference in the kinds of stories you report and how you look while reporting them. We call it *news karma.* The same goes for everyone with a hand in putting the news on the air. Make waves, you sink. Make friends and sail on.

It's a small world. You never know where someone will end up. Today's interns are tomorrow's news directors. A great reporter with a lot of talent could never get into the station he really wanted to. He'd interned with someone who ended up becoming the news director at that station just a few years later. The two didn't mesh, and that was that. This isn't to say you have to be nice to everybody. It's just some food for thought.

A reporter in a medium-sized market effectively shut down all job opportunities for a former news director she'd interviewed with in a small market. The ND had told the reporter that she had no talent and to give up the job-hunting. The reporter went on to bigger and better things. When she saw the ND's resumé tape on her own ND's desk for an open reporter position, she told her own ND not to hire her. He ended up throwing out the tape. The former ND could have avoided this by being diplomatic, and encouraging, maybe giving the reporter some pointers in job-hunting. It never hurts to help.

FILE IT HERE

Probably the most dreaded types of days you'll have in a newsroom are the "slow news days." Nothing's going on. You still need to fill the same amount of time. If you're an assignment editor, this is the worst. You have to come up with story ideas. This is where the contacts come in. You call everyone you know. After all the voice-mail messages have been returned to no avail, and all your follow-ups have turned up nothing, what now? This is where the story file comes in, and boy, will it come in handy.

What do you put in it? Just about anything you come across that could possibly be a story, newspaper clippings, magazine articles, AP news copy, e-mails, whatever. It's great, and it will be more valuable than you know. Just take a little time when you have time and you'll avoid the panic of not having anything to fill the show with. It's something good to do when you have that extra few minutes when the scanners are quiet, the phones have stopped ringing, and you can actually take a few relaxed breaths.

Everyone in the newsroom is expected to contribute story ideas. And, not just any story ideas. News managers want "lead" story ideas. Reporters, make it a point to know your stuff. Keep as up to date as possible on the local big stories, so you can walk into the editorial meeting confident that you have the idea to lead the newscasts. And, just in case it's a "slow news day," have your own files, too. Photographers, generate your ideas from talking to people out in the field. Producers, think of follow-ups that you didn't have time to do the first time around. These individual story files are essentially the compilation of the personalities and experiences in the newsroom. Use them to dig up the best "lead" stories and to cover your back on the dreaded "slow news day."

TALK TO THE BIG GUNS

This is a tough one. Especially on your first job. You're working so hard to prove yourself, whatever your job, that you ignore the people who hired you. You don't mean to. It just happens. But don't let it. Take time out and knock on your news director's door. Bring with you a tape of your work, samples of your writing, or a list of stories you've generated and look it over together. Ask questions. How am I doing? What am I doing right? What needs improvement? Get specifics and forge an understanding of what's expected of you. By keeping an open line of communication with the bosses you stand a better chance of staying in their good graces. Remember, they hired you. They can fire you.

Probably one of the hardest things to take is the lack of communication from above, especially the big bosses outside of the newsroom. If you don't make a move to see what they're thinking, you may never know until your contract isn't renewed. Most will probably appreciate your willingness to ask for feedback. It's important. Countless news people are kept in the dark about their job performances until evaluation time. And you don't want to hear from the producer that the big boss upstairs is unhappy with your performance. Go directly to the source.

"Good photographers and reporters need to work as a team . . . a reporter needs to think like a photographer and a photographer needs to think like a reporter. They need to talk about story focus. That way they both bring something to the table."

Eric Kehe, photographer

GO TEAM

We said before that a newscast can't make it to air without the entire team, like a baseball team with only six or seven players. And it's true. You won't last long in a newsroom where you're the eighth or ninth player who's not playing ball.

Here's a situation for you. After a long day, a reporter has finished a live newsroom hit and is waiting for the show to end before going home. Suddenly, breaking news. Should the reporter leave the newsroom or volunteer to go cover the breaking news? The news director would say, the team player pitches in. Which is what the reporter should do. Pitch in and head to the scene. That goes for all those working in a newsroom. Don't put yourself above the dirty work like writing last-minute stories or running late scripts to anchors, or even pulling cables. And, don't wait to be asked. Jump in and get it done. Not only will you learn more about a lot of things that help put the news on the air, but you'll gain a go-to reputation and respect (especially from the managers).

Think about it this way: the person with the most information wins. If you're out there, doing any job that needs to be done, who will become one of the most important people in the newsroom? Who will everyone (again, especially managers) call upon when there's breaking news, and things need to get done, get done right, and get done right away? Right again. There's nothing that can boost your confidence more than knowing exactly what's going on, what to do next, and knowing you're indispensable. On the flip side, there's nothing worse than having people busily working all around you, and you sitting in the eye of the hurricane not knowing what to do. Don't think people won't notice.

"You're not special just because someone puts you in front of a camera to tell a story. You're only part of a team of professionals who are really at the service of the story."
Michael Moffett, freelance producer-reporter

UNDER PRESSURE

This is a given, if you haven't figured that out already. Nearly every second of your working day will be on a deadline, no matter what your specific job. The clock is ticking until news time. You must remain calm. It's not easy. But it is necessary. A lot can happen in a few seconds and how you react is crucial. Suddenly, the teleprompter goes black. The anchors can panic and fumble. Or, they can carry on with their hard copy scripts. The producer can either flip out or find an engineer to find the problem and fix it. Keeping your cool is one of the best things you can do for yourself and your career. So meditate, exercise, breath deeply, or find a secluded corner to scream. Whatever works for you, use it. You can't think clearly if you're in a frenzy. Trust us on this one.

Probably one of the best things to do when you're under pressure is to stay focused. It's so easy to think about what can happen if things fall apart. Don't go there. If you're a reporter, keep writing your story, or find a way to wrap it up quickly so you make deadline (this is where learning the system and learning to write concisely will come in handy). What if you're live and your package gets stuck in the machine? Will you be able to succinctly tell the story live if this happens? Assignment editors, keep phone numbers you need in an orderly file or other system, so you can start making calls without getting flustered. Don't get frustrated with nonhelpful PIOs. Many have never been trained to talk to media and are afraid to say anything. Remember, being rude to them just won't help. Ask as many questions as you can, and get the information quickly to the producer or the reporter. Producers, keep a backup plan in your head at all times. This way you'll know what to do if that live shot goes down at the last minute. Will the reporter have enough time to come back to the station and do an on-set piece instead? Keep tabs on the weather. Nothing says danger like a thunderstorm during a live shot. Anchors, be aware of your surroundings, too. If you hear that a live shot may have some problems, gear yourself up for the worst-case scenario, and you'll be prepared. And editors, look at the rundown, so you know how to prioritize the stories you're editing. Don't edit the kicker, the last story in the show, before the lead story, if you have both at your disposal now. If you get into a crunch, again, stay focused. You don't want your lack of concentration to leave a big black hole in a reporter's story because you forgot to cover it with video.

Some people love the pressure. There are some reporters who actually perform better on live shots under severe pressure than on a leisurely day. Make pressure work for you. Sometimes, it can even be fun!

ROLL WITH THE PUNCHES

Short and simple. But it's the hardest thing to do. Work at learning to take criticism with a smile. No two people in the newsroom, especially your managers, will have the same opinion about you or your work. And, when they do criticize your performance, remember that it's one person's opinion. Listen to what they say, but don't immediately take it to heart. You wouldn't allow any single thing anyone says to shape how you live your life. So, why stand for it at work? The trick is to take in all the criticism and look for commonalities. If eight out of ten people say you could use more energy in your live shots, chances are you could use more energy in your live shots. Make the criticism work for you. And, remember, don't dish it out if you can't take it.

Criticism may be the one thing that destroys newsroom camaraderie faster than anything. Don't fall into this trap. It's easy to criticize others. But remember, all those other folks will be the first to take you on and watch for you to make a mistake. We all make mistakes, but it's how you handle them that really counts.

And it's not just on-air talent that set themselves up for criticism. Sure, talent have an added dimension that people can make fun of, their appearance, along with their job performance. So you need to have an extra thick skin. People will make fun of your hair, your lipstick color, your receding hairline, you name it. Just try to take it all with a sense of humor. After all, the color of lipstick you wear doesn't determine what kind of journalist you are.

Assignment editors and producers, you'll get criticism for the decisions you make, because you'll be the ones making constant choices. Do I send a crew here or there, or do I drop that story and add this one?

What shall my lead be? Keep in mind the reasons why you make the decisions you do . . . and even if someone criticizes you, at least you'll know why you did what you did and can feel confident that you did the right thing with the information you had on hand, or can learn from the mistake. You'll be the better journalist in the end and survive the bad times.

> Don't share information! Check it out! Check it out again!

EXCLUSIVE INFORMATION

With few exceptions, the cardinal rule of TV news is, "Don't share information!" Do your own legwork. Ask your own questions. Don't rely on other reporters to fill you in on what's happening. How do you know that what they say is accurate or even true? Trust us. You'll earn your colleagues' respect faster and keep it longer if you stick to the facts you dug up. If you rely on someone else's information, and it is wrong, will you want to take responsibility for that? How do you explain *that* to the boss? Keeping your ears open and knowing a lot about the community and the world around you can help prevent your falling behind on a story. It will happen to you, but don't panic. Using your head will help out in the end. There's nothing wrong with getting a tip, or overhearing competitors talking about something. But, *check it out* first!

However, there is a time to share. If you're all at a press conference, and a competitor's camera battery goes dead, lend one of yours. Or share lights; not everyone has to set up lights for the same interview. The old saying, "what goes around comes around," really applies here. One day, it will be your camera or mic battery that dies right before a major press conference announcement. It's a strange dichotomy, but with all the competition there is still that camaraderie to help each other out in times of need. And there will definitely be a time of need for everyone at some point.

NUMBERS, NUMBERS,
AND MORE NUMBERS

Your Rolodex will save your life. We know this from experience. Remember how we told you to compile a Rolodex even before you started work? Don't let it end there. Get a card or a name and phone number from everyone you meet. Or simply store their number in your cell phone. From the senator to the tarot card reader, each contact is valuable, no matter how obscure they may seem. Who knows, maybe one day that senator will make a decision based on her tarot card readings. And guess who that psychic will call with the exclusive information?

Pass out plenty of your cards, too. Every once in a while it pays off with someone calling with a great story. Gaining trust and respect from the everyday people you meet in the field, or talk to on the phone, will pay off. When an average Joe has a great news story and wants to call someone "on TV," he'll remember you and you'll get the goods.

RUNDOWN? WHAT RUNDOWN?

The rundown is the blueprint of the show. Take a look at the sample we've included here.

Does it look confusing? Once we sort it all out for you, you'll see exactly why the rundown keeps the show together. Each line, each slug is a different story. A different tape format. A different camera shot. A different anchor reading the intro. It's the producer's bible and the reporter's guide to how and when their story airs. Editors can look at it and see where the story they are editing airs, and can prioritize. Assignment editors need to know what aired during the evening newscast to see if there are any follow-ups. And when there's a big story, everyone will be enlightened. Are there several angles to the same overall big story, like a flash flood? As a reporter, are you doing the overall story of what happened, or the story on the clean-up, or maybe the story on a grandmother who saved her grandchild? Whichever one you're assigned to, you need to know what airs before and after you. If you're after the main story, don't

SAMPLE RUNDOWN

PAGE	TAL	SHOT	STORY SLUG	FORMAT	WRT	TIME
	E/M	2SHT	PRESHOW:	VO/ VO/ SOTVO	CM	0:30
			-OPEN-	VTR		0:20
A1	E/M	WIPE	COLD OPEN	VONAT	CM	0:20
	E/M	2SHT	GOOD EVENING	RDR		0:05
A2	ES	SS	DUI CRACKDOWN LD		RT	0:15
	E/R	LIVE BOXES				
A3	RT	SAT	TOSS TO CRACKDOWN PKG	VO/GX	RT	0:20
A4	—	WIPE	DUI CRACKDOWN PKG	PKG	RT	1:10
A5	RT	SAT	TOSS TO SET	RDR	RT	0:10
	E/R	LIVE BOXES				
A6	ES	OTS	DUI STATS	GX	RT	0:15
A7	ML	OTS	HOLIDAY TRAFFIC	N/V/S	CC	0:25
A8	EMK	3SHT	TOSS TO HOLIDAY WX	RDR	CC	0:10
A9	KT	SS	HOLIDAY WX	RDR	KT	1:10
A10	KT	WX	WX GRX	WALL	KT	
A11	KT	WIPE	ANNUAL SNOWFALL	VO/GX	KT	
A12	ML	OTS	EL NINO?	N/V/S	GS	0:30
A13	ES	OTS	WATER RESTRICTIONS	GX	GS	0:20
A20	E/M	2SHT	SUPER TZ	VO		2:00
			TZ 1A: SHOOTING FOLO	SOTVO		
	JH	LIVE	TZ 1B: LIVE TEASE/FIRE UPDATE	LIVE		
	E/M	WIPE	TZ 1C: GOOD SAMARITIAN	SOT		
	JS	SPX	TZ 1D: SPX AHEAD	NATVO		
	JH	LIVE	LIVE TEASE/WX	WX SHOT		
			—BREAK 1A———————BREAK 1A—			3:00

put in how the flood happened . . . the reporter before you just said that. Editors, which video has already been used, so viewers don't see the same shot three times in five minutes?

On paper, this is how the show is going to go. So, it's important to learn to know what it all means.

Let's go through this now with our sample rundown:

Starting on the top row: the page numbers are important because it's so easy to refer to something right away, especially if your director has a question (i.e., "On page A3 is the reporter using a splitscreen graphic?"). The reason why the numbering skips to A20 for the tease is so the producer can add in pages as needed without renumbering the last page in the block, which is always the tease.

Talent, of course, is who's on camera at the time. E/M means that both anchors, Ellie and Mark, are on a two-shot.

Story slug is the name of the story. WX is short for weather, AX means accident, GRX means graphic. Toss means that the reporter is live, leading into his/her package, and then doing a live tag out of the package, and "tossing" back to the anchors at the newsdesk.

Format is straightforward; GRX means a graphic, wall means the weather anchor is at the weather wall, N/V/S is NAT VO/SOT, which is a piece of tape that starts with natural sound, with video, then goes to a bite. Some stations do this on one continuous tape, so the talent will have to time it out exactly to the bite, and others do this on two or even three separate pieces of tape, one for the VO, the second for the SOT, the third for a tag.

WRT is writer. Who wrote the story? Who can the producer go to with a question?

TIME is approximately how long it takes to cover that particular story or read. The "good evening" page by the anchors is short, just five seconds. Packages are usually between one minute and two minutes; VOs should hardly ever be longer than thirty seconds, or the audience will get bored. The tease is a long one here, with a lot of elements, a live reporter, the sports anchor, and the weather anchor, so it takes two minutes. The commercial break in this case is three minutes.

Once you learn to read your station's rundown, you'll never be at a loss for the status of what's going on. As an assignment editor, you'll know which stories the producer has selected to put in the show; yes, she wants a follow-up on that shooting, so you'll need to make that call. Photographers will know where their story falls in the show, and if it comes down to the wire, how much time to air. Editors know which stories have priority, which to pull file for, and how much time is allotted for each. Reporters will know where they are in the show, if they have a live tease, and how much time they have to tell their stories. Producers, this is your blueprint for every second of the newscast, literally.

Learn the rundown and live by it, every day. There's no faster way of getting information about the newscast than simply calling up the rundown on the computer.

WHAT IF?

It's your first day on the job. The boss says you should take the day to get adjusted, make calls, and learn the computer system. The other reporters are out on stories when suddenly the assignment desk gets word of a school bus crash with injured children on the scene. You're the only one who can go. How would you handle this situation?

Or, it's a couple of weeks into the new job and you're getting used to your new surroundings. You're finishing up work on your story about changes in local fire codes for government buildings. Then, the police and fire scanners start going crazy. There's been a shooting at a local school. The newsroom is chaotic. It's crisis mode time. Everyone seems to know just what to do to help, except you. What would you do?

DO WHAT WE'D DO

We can sum up our advice on how to react in both of these situations in two words: Pitch in.

In the case of the school bus crash on your first day, just dive in headfirst. Before you leave for the crash scene find out what the assignment desk knows—injuries, deaths, number of vehicles involved. Keep in mind, though, that reports over the scanner aren't always accurate. Also, find out if there is a police or rescue contact for you to call or hook up with on the scene. Then go! But never lose contact with the station, if at all possible. They may be able to feed you vital new information you'll need to navigate your way through your first big breaking news story.

When you get to the scene, observe what other reporters are doing. Take a pointer from the photographer, who's probably done this many times before. He or she can help you gather information and clue you in as to who to talk to at the scene. (Assignment editors, if you have a green reporter, try to match them up with a seasoned photographer; this can save time and grief later on.) Find an "official" and ask questions, the big six: who, what, where, when, why, and how.

Can you interview the kids who were on the bus? You can, but you may need their parent's permission before you air them. We'll talk more about legal situations in chapter 10.

In a major crisis, as in the second example, remain calm and find a way to help. Start making calls to police, offer to pair up with a photographer and head toward the school, or just offer to be a gatekeeper of information. In these situations organization of information is imperative. There are no hard and fast rules. Just get in there and help get the job done, however you can.

If you must talk over the two-way to field crews, or back to the station, don't spill the beans. Other stations can hear everything you say. If you're onto something and don't have a cell phone, call from a land line, which is a pay phone.

6

THE BUSINESS OF NEWS

THE BOTTOM LINE

The bottom line is that news is a business. And no business will stay in business if it doesn't make money. That's why there is so much pressure to bring in good ratings, and why ratings periods are so important from a business standpoint.

You all know that advertising is the way stations, networks, and conglomerates make their money. And with such fierce competition between cable and satellite TV, profit margins are getting thinner as the wealth is spread around.

That means that advertising and the sales department are all-important in any station. Here's a fact of life: Sales makes the money, news spends the money. News doesn't make the money, so therefore it can be dictated to by those departments that do. This will never change.

So, how does that affect you as an assignment editor, a producer, or an on-air talent? You'd think that the sales people are there to worry about making the money and that managers and administrators are there to worry about spending the money, so you, as a journalist, would be way out of the loop. This is just not true.

Ever wonder why you rarely see a negative news story about car companies, or local car dealerships? Sit down and watch any show for just one commercial break and you'll see why. How many national car ads do you see (i.e., an ad for a specific make of car, like Cadillac or Ford trucks, etc.)? How many for a local car dealer (i.e., "Come on down, we'll take anything you can push, pull, or drag in!!!")? Automobile sales make up a good portion of ads you see on television.

And keeping that in mind, this could be a likely situation at your station:

You get a news tip from a caller that a local low-end, but popular, car dealership in town is rolling back the odometers on cars for sale. You happen to know a mechanic, and you take a car out for a test drive. While you're out, you have your friend check out the odometer. Bingo! It's been rolled back. You're excited about getting the newsroom to give you the go-ahead to do this exclusive. Your suggestion is met with less than enthusiasm. In fact, it's flatly rejected by your news director. Why?

Simple. Money. And your boss(es) may or may not be straight with you about this point. It's amazing how quickly ads can be pulled from a station, even at the first hint of a negative news story. Even before it's aired. And those ads can add up to big bucks. Big advertisers control a lot of news content. Period.

CASE IN POINT

A news producer in a medium-sized market was doing a segment on fat content in fast-food products. It's no secret, but the point was to show just how much fat certain products contain. A nutritionist was the guest, and to prove his point, he brought a blender. He put a hamburger and fries in it, blended it up, and out came all the fat. To say the least, it was a very visual demonstration of the fat content in this particular fast food product. As soon as the segment aired, that particular advertiser was on the phone to the station, pulled their ads for six months, and in the end, the producer got a good talking-to, with a stern reminder to make sure that it didn't happen again.

This is a legitimate story that affects everyone . . . most of us eat fast food, and know it contains fat, but we don't truly realize just how much until we see it. This was an actual news-you-can-use story. But its news value was overridden by The Bottom Line.

> "(I made) $9,500 as a morning anchor/reporter (1981). If any-
> one beats my first salary I'd like to know. I'll send them my
> condolences!"
>
> Tom Hanson, anchor

YOUR PAYCHECK

How much will you get paid on your first job? It will vary from
market to market, job to job, and even station to station within the
same market. And many times even the same position in the same
station won't be compensated equally, for a variety of reasons. Don't
look for big salaries. A starting salary of around $20,000 a year is
probably what you'll be looking at. As an assignment editor, producer, writer, or photographer, you probably won't make much
money for a long time. Reporters most likely won't. Anchoring is
obviously where the money is, in large markets, anyway. But not
everyone can be the star. It's like a professional sports team. There
are those few "stars" that make the big bucks, but the other players
and the coaches won't even come close, even though your roles are
just as important. Get used to it. As we've said often enough, if you
get into this career for money or glamour, you'll probably get out
pretty quickly. That's why a love of the job is so important, like
teaching, because the salaries just don't compensate you for all the
things you do and are responsible for on a daily basis.

Remember, TV news is a business, and one of your news director's responsibilities, among many, is to keep the newsroom budget as
low as possible while keeping the product quality as high as possible.
Some stations have a high commitment to news, which is good financially, because generally, those stations will pay more to get and keep
good people. A station that feels that news is just something it has to
have is probably not going to have the highest salary scale in the market. On the other hand, there is probably less pressure there to perform. It's all in how the station determines how the newsroom fits
into its business plan.

ADD IT UP

Exactly how does the station make money? Well, it's a complicated business, based on ratings . . . so basically, we can say that the viewing habits of a miniscule number of people determine what you see and hear each day.

It works this way. Stations have the traditional ratings periods, which are February, May, July, and November. The "sweeps," or "books," determine programming and changes of programming for the following months. Larger television markets subscribe to "overnights," which are ratings determined each night and broken down into each quarter of an hour. They come out every morning. The overnights gauge how well shows and newscasts are doing. But the sweeps determine what the "demos" are, that is, what types of people are watching certain programs. For instance, newscasts try to

Sweeps

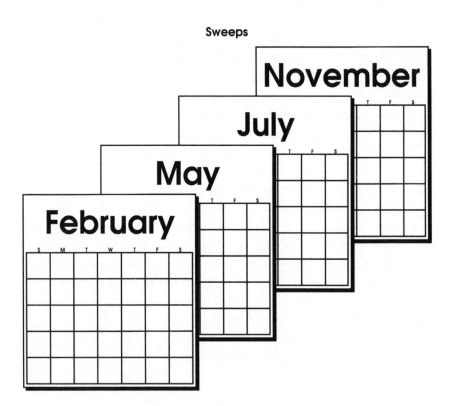

attract the prime demographics, people ages 18–49. Those are the folks that sales departments consider the most lucrative, with the most spending power.

RATINGS = $$$$

Ratings are everything. They determine how popular a show or program is, and that popularity, in turn, can determine how much a station will charge for each program. This may be a surprise to you, but there is only one service out there that measures ratings: Nielsen. Ratings are determined either by people writing in diaries what they've watched, or by electronic boxes placed on people's TVs, electronically tallying what is watched.

Either way, those ratings directly relate to how much a station charges for advertising spots during a certain program or time period. Obviously, prime time (the time between the evening news broadcast and the nighttime news broadcast) can garner the most money, because more people are watching. That's why you see the cheesy commercials overnight, because stations charge a bare minimum for those spots.

A station has the right to reject any spot for any reason, whether it's due to sexual content, violence, or whatever. On the flip side, stations aren't held liable for the content of the spots . . . for instance, you can't sue a station for running a spot on a diet supplement that later turns out to be a health hazard.

Ratings: A percentage of all television households in a certain market.
Share: The percentage of television households turned on watching a particular program.

LEARN THE LINGO

To understand how ratings are measured, and how much of a science this has become, you need to know the lingo.

- **HUT:** Households using television
- **PUT:** Persons using television
- **Golden Triangle:** This is the five-minute period after each quarter-hour, i.e., :00 to :05, :15 to :20, :30 to :35, etc. Ratings really only measure the first five minutes of the quarter hour. You win that, you win the quarter hour. So, news producers are asked to make sure that commercials aren't running during those times (viewers tend to turn away during the commercial break). Those times are theoretically set for great stories or teases to keep the viewers tuned in for that all-important five minutes.

Golden Triangle

CROSS-PROMOTION AND SALES

This is something no journalist is really crazy about, but it's something that you've got to get used to. Cross-promotion means that the sales department is promoting something, usually a program, and wants the news department to do a tie-in, so that folks watching the news will tune into the other programming at the station too. Arguably, successful news departments, with high ratings, tend to have more cross-promotion.

It's free advertising for the station's programs. Since networks have to run a certain amount of promotion for programming (hence losing advertising spots they could have run), this is a valuable sales tool. And face it, there is no or very little actual news value to these types of stories.

For instance, if you're with a network affiliate, and it's the season premiere of a popular series, then you might be assigned to do a story about the show's central issue. Or, if an upcoming episode of a popular medical drama deals with a strange illness, you might do a story on that type of illness in your town. And on and on.

Be cautious when sales hands you a story to do. Yeah, it will sound great . . . because it's a sales pitch. A lot of times you won't have a choice whether to run a story, set up a story, or do a story that sales has "suggested." But you do have control over whether you did it right and got the other side. We admit, it's a tough line to walk. Sales won't want anything negative said about a client of theirs. On the other hand, you're hired by the newsroom to be ethical, and you have an obligation to your viewers. You wouldn't want to do a really positive story on diet supplements, using only the client, and someone who's lost 106 pounds, only to find out a few months down the road that the supplement is being taken off the shelves because it has been found to cause adverse health effects. Especially as a reporter, your face is on that story. Your obligation is to talk to a doctor or a nutritionist about use of the supplement. Your viewing audience isn't stupid, and they'll remember. There's hardly an easier way to lose credibility.

You as a reporter will be asked to do these stories, as an assignment editor you will be asked to set up these stories, and as a producer you will be asked to put these stories into your show lineup. And your managers will most likely be supportive. As we said earlier, your managers report to their bosses, and generally station managers come from a sales background.

Is this journalistic integrity at its finest? Of course not. Will these stories further your news career? Not likely. But these situations are unavoidable. The bread has to be buttered somewhere. Once again, get used to it. The best thing to do is bite your tongue, smile, and get through it. Either way, it's not likely to change the world.

THE BOTTOM LINE ABOUT THE BOTTOM LINE

During ratings there are no vacations, personal days, and even sick days are frowned upon. You're expected to be there and do your best work ever. Remember, the entire station's earnings hinge upon the "book." So, put your life on hold and don't plan any vacation time until the book is over. The upside, though, is that more resources may be dedicated to stories for series promotion, like an exposé on teens, designer drugs, and rave parties. Or the undercover investigation into the city worker drunk on the job and on the taxpayer dime.

Also, ratings periods can be high-anxiety time, too. For anchors, a few bad books can mean an early end to a long-term contract. For assignment editors, there is extra pressure to get every spot news story. A manager doesn't like seeing a story on the other stations that you didn't get. For producers, there's that added pressure to keep the shows lively, full of energy, and watchable without any errors. Nothing puts a news manager in a grumpy mood faster than a bad book. His job is on the line, too.

Ratings can wreak havoc with the way you do your jobs. In many ways your daily jobs will hinge on the ratings from the night before. Entire newscasts may be restructured to garner what the managers believe will be bigger ratings. It's not an exact science by any means. But it's a fact of newsroom life.

THEY CALL IT "CONVERGENCE"

Another fact of newsroom life is convergence. It is and will likely remain a news management buzzword for years. Simply put, it refers to the integration of all news and information sources through emerging technologies. The idea is that one day we'll be able to get our news and entertainment, surf the web, shop, communicate . . . live our lives through personal computers (whatever form they may take). Technological convergence is already happening, in the form of:

- Cell phones that are digital cameras, (like the ones TV reporters use to cover war stories, when a lot of gear can be a major drawback), and that can dial up the worldwide web, or even be used to buy soft drinks with from vending machines;
- Home entertainment systems that combine TV, radio, CD, DVD, and home computer;
- Cars and trucks equipped with global positioning satellite (GPS) systems, computers, telephones, and televisions.

Now, television news and the news industry, in general, are scrambling to catch up. Newspapers, radio, and television stations are combining resources to make sure their names and their news are everywhere consumers look. From the nightly news to the morning headlines, to the worldwide web . . . the new, converging business of news is changing fast. Probably the most visible manifestation would be "print" reporters appearing in "television" newscasts.

"*Post* Business Reporter Stacy Mills is live from the *Post* newsroom with more on what record unemployment means to the city's long-term economy. . . ." Incidentally, you may ask why a TV station would rely on a print reporter for information when they have plenty of their own reporters on staff. Well, the truth of the matter is that many print reporters are specialists in their field. Newspapers have many more reporters on their staffs than television stations do. They have more time to dig deeper and learn. They need to, because a 9-inch column requires a lot more information than a 1:30 package. They aren't really hampered by technology, such as shooting, editing, and so on. They can make calls and write. So this trend is expected to continue.

Another example of convergence is television weathercasters recording drive-time forecasts for radio. "This is KWXX-TV Meteorologist Mike Sunshine. Expect a high in the low 70's today. . . ." Why hire a staff meteorologist when you can use someone else's? And reap the benefits of cross-promotion and that TV weatherperson's credibility at the same time? Makes business sense.

Or, look at streaming video on the Internet. "Catch complete election coverage live, on-line with Eyewitness News.com. . . ."

Future news convergence can and will further distort the traditional news lines. As media powerhouses continue to buy up television, radio, and print interests around the world, look for more sharing of resources, sources, and people. The challenge for you will be your ability to roll with the punches and adapt. Assignment editors may be working for several newsrooms. Producers may write for Internet, radio, cable, and broadcast television. Anchors, reporters, and photographers . . . get ready for more than the next show, shoot, or live shot.

And, in another sense, convergence means more pressure for journalists. Pressure to get it on the air, and on the web, first. Pressure to get it right. These pressures are not always compatible. Remember, with convergence, the information you collect won't just be on TV. It'll be on the web, maybe fed to newsrooms your station owns across the country, attributed in the newspaper, on the radio, and whatever else the technology world happens to develop.

Take for instance, the war with Iraq. During the Gulf War in 1991, many newsrooms sent their own reporters to Kuwait or other Middle Eastern areas to report what was going on, especially if service people at their local military bases were sent to a certain location. Now, there's no need. Networks will take care of that. However, the pressure is on the network reporter, whose information will be delivered to the entire country, and around the world to anyone with a satellite dish or an Internet connection. Whatever he/she reports has *got* to be correct. The era of local reporters going overseas, or to cover national events is drawing to an end. Just one reporter will cover these stories for many stations in the network, and in turn, for the newspapers these stations are "connected" with, and for their collective Internet sites as well.

Convergence means more news for consumers. The problem is, the business of news means fewer people will be doing more to deliver it. The truth about convergence for journalists, no matter how it pans out, is be ready to do more with less for the same money. Learn all you can about other positions in your newsroom, and other media formats. And, brush up on those computer skills. You'll most likely be needing these in the near future.

Money talks, ratings count, news goes on.

7

CROSSING THE LINE

News ethics are tricky business. One of the hardest things about news is something you'll be asked to do every single day: separate yourself from the story. That includes distancing your feelings about the people and politics you cover from the stories you do concerning these issues. It's not easy. A good way to know if you've covered a particularly sticky issue as fairly as possible is if you get caller complaints from both sides of the story.

The reason why this is so hard is that nobody is brought up in a vacuum. We all have certain ways of looking at things, sometimes without knowing it. And we can't help but bring these with us to each story we cover. Knowing about these and learning to set them aside is the best way to be as fair as you can on every story you do.

The great thing about working in a newsroom is that it forces you to become more open-minded. You'll talk to people you would never have met otherwise. And many of those people are completely different from you—from super rich to devastatingly poor to very powerful or very famous. Open your mind, learn from each person

> "I always tell my people to never do anything you'd be ashamed of, anything that you'd have to cover your tracks for. It's simple. Just tell the truth."
>
> Mona Dyer, news director

and situation, and you'll be a much better journalist for it. A richer, fuller person, too.

THIS JUST IN

When somebody calls you with a news tip, listen closely. Write down everything they say. A lot of times, "tips" sound great . . . you're going to get an exclusive, and right a wrong in the process. The fact of the matter is, that most people who call news stations have their own point of view, and most of these so-called "tips" are generally from someone disgruntled about one thing or another. After checking out the other side, 90 percent of these tips will not pan out. But take each one seriously, especially if you work on an assignment desk and are answering phones much of the time. Eventually one will come along that will be exactly what you're looking for.

> Remember, everyone has a motive for asking you to do a story. Always keep it in mind when you do the story, and in finding out the other side.

The best ally you'll have going for you in any situation is to be skeptical. Understand that anyone who actively seeks out airtime has some sort of motivation. Ascertaining what that motivation is isn't always easy. But once you've done that, you'll be better equipped to deal with the story, if you do one at all.

Example: Someone calls the station saying he has a tip about a dangerous situation near a schoolyard. The caller says his neighbor has vicious dogs that are allowed to run around the neighborhood, and he is especially concerned about the school kids that walk by every day, even though he doesn't have kids of his own. This call comes at a time when two other children have been hospitalized because of dog bites on the way home from school. This could be good. What do you do, how do you check this out?

Start by making calls. Call the school in the neighborhood. Has anyone there heard any complaints from kids or parents about dogs running loose? Many news stations now have a cross-reference software system that allows you to call neighbors of a certain address. If you're still unsure, see if any photographers or even a crew is out in that area. Ask them to stop by and check it out.

ON THE SCENE

You are the reporter nearby and are asked to go by the scene. It's a great time, too, since school is just about to let out. Observe what happens. The desk calls you back and has scheduled an interview with the caller, let's call him Joe. Even before the camera starts rolling, Joe is talking about the neighborhood, how it's not friendly, and how the people next door are the worst. You start getting the feeling that something else is going on here.

When the camera rolls, you ask about the dogs. Joe says those dogs are driving him crazy, that they bark constantly. You've heard nothing since you've been there, and ask him where the dogs are now. He says he doesn't know, but it's the first time all day that they've been quiet. Wrap up the interview, and go for the neighbors next. The neighbors don't have any complaints about the dogs. You ask to interview their kids. The kids say the same. Neighbors all say the man who called you is a nut, people stay away from him, and that all he does is complain about the dogs next door. One neighbor tells you Joe wants a fence between the properties for privacy, but doesn't want to foot the bill.

End of story . . . the guy really dislikes his neighbor, and just wants his own privacy. His motivation isn't about the kids walking by at all . . . the guy just wants a fence built between the properties and doesn't want to pay for half, and hopes the media pressure will do the trick. At this point, you don't need to find out about the disagreements with the neighborhood, just politely say thanks and leave. Sometimes this is what it takes to *not* do a story. It was worth checking out. The other side of the story is usually just as interesting, although not always something that should make it to air. Chalk these types of situations up to experience.

DON'T USE IT, OR LOSE IT

This is an easy one. Don't use your job or position to gain freebies. For starters, you're representing your entire station, and the entire news business to folks who've never met a reporter, assignment editor, photographer, or producer before.

And it can get you into trouble. Example: A reporter, new on the job in a small market, (where reporters can be big fish in small ponds), has car trouble. He takes the car to a mechanic. When he looks at the bill, he's upset. He tells the mechanic that he's been cheated, and oh, by the way, he works at the local station and could really get some negative coverage out of this for the mechanic. By the time the reporter gets into his car, and arrives at the station, he's almost asked to pack up his desk. Why? The mechanic had called the station, talked to the general manager, and lodged a complaint. Working for a TV station doesn't always gain you leverage with local business. If you have a legitimate complaint, be like anybody else. Check it out, check for other complaints, and lodge a complaint in more conventional channels. In all probability, the business owner buys commercial airtime at your station, and you'll really get someone mad.

Be smart about what's right. Using your press pass to get into local events shouldn't happen, but it does, and most likely everyone has done it sometime in their careers, especially at the beginning, when money is a precious commodity. Doing this all the time will label you as the Freebie Seeker from your station, and it's more humiliating than it's worth. Remember, a press pass isn't a free ticket. Now, there's a difference if you're checking something out to see if it's worth a story. Or to add to a story. It's easier to tell folks about the great new aquarium if you've been through the exhibit and can add to what aquarium visitors have to say. But don't wear out your welcome and bring five family members and your girlfriend. It's just cheesy.

Further, know when not to participate. If you're doing a story about a new ride opening at the local amusement park, park the press pass. Your viewers will think you scammed a ride just for the fun of it. And you did. This time, let other riders do the talking. Really, nobody cares how much fun *you* had doing the story. A good rule of thumb that some reporters and anchors just don't get: *it's not about you!*

Almost every station will have you sign what's called a payola agreement. It means that you cannot accept any type of gift over a certain amount, which varies from station to station. Some stations won't allow you to accept anything over $25. Therefore, you could accept a pair of movie tickets but not rock concert tickets.

Some will have what some stations term a "plugola" agreement, which means you can't give a certain company or product a free "plug" on air in return for money or free products or services.

> "When you are in a situation where a tragedy has occurred, be respectful of the victims and their families, know when to put the camera down, or when to move away. I've hugged more than one crying mother in my day. I've let paramedics use my light to treat a car crash victim. Some pictures can wait, you have to be a human being first."
>
> Carol Lynde, photographer

TALKING TO VICTIMS

This should be a no-brainer. Victims or their family members don't ask for this. It's one of the worst times of their lives. Frankly, it's surprising how many victims or their relatives do talk to the media. Some hope that by telling others their story, what happened to them can be prevented from happening to other people. But many others probably just don't have the willpower or the right frame of mind to say "no." And others don't think they have the option.

A mother of a student at Columbine High School says she was dogged by a network news producer who wouldn't allow her child to attend a prayer vigil until the producer determined that the interview he was conducting with the student was over. This was an interview that was taking place in the student's home. What would you do in this situation? Simply not allow the student to attend the vigil, just a day or so after the shootings, when emotion is running high? Or go back to your bosses and tell them you didn't get everything they had asked for? How about checking ahead of time, and telling the family this may take awhile. If you discover your time is short, ask the most pertinent questions up front. That way, anything from there on out is gravy, and you haven't intruded too much on this family's life. Or maybe ask the student if you can go to the prayer vigil, too, and get the student's reaction.

Families of anyone who went to Columbine, regardless of whether they knew any of the victims or not, were at times hounded and harassed. In another case, one producer was literally pulling an interviewee away from another producer for a live hit. This was at 5 A.M. There is a lot of pressure in these situations to perform, but keep in mind that the people you need, that is, those whom you are interviewing, are people, not commodities. If you need someone right away for a live shot, ask them politely, and explain it's urgent. Grabbing someone by the sleeve and dragging them along with you is not the best way to put someone at ease, especially if they are being asked to go live on national television. At the time, things are so urgent, and people are crabby. But in the end, these are not life-and-death situations. As much as many of us hate to admit it, we aren't brain surgeons. We don't save lives. We just make them more interesting.

Keep in mind that people you interview are *people*. Since interviewing is something reporters, assignment editors, and some producers do every day, it's easy to forget that these soundbites you need are actually real people with feelings and considerations. Be a better journalist, and bear this in mind every time you make the call, knock on the door, or approach someone on-scene.

"Follow the golden rule. Treat people like you'd want to be treated, even difficult people. Remember that we're thrusting a camera and a mic in their face. You don't have to agree with them, just be fair."

Patti Dennis, vice president/news director

The power we hold as journalists shouldn't be underestimated. Viewers depend on us, trust us, to be truthful and ethical. Sometimes living up to that, combined with the pressures of competition and ratings, can cloud the issue.

On the flip side, you're a person too. It's not too hard to get wrapped up in a story. But remember you aren't part of it. Take the case of a woman who fought off an attacker in her apartment. Every reporter in town wanted to talk to her, but understandably she was afraid. The woman did return the call of one of the reporters, whom she felt she could trust, and they set up an interview. She inadvertently told a competing reporter that she was already talking to someone else, and only to that person. The second reporter ended up getting the interview, after inferring that the first reporter wouldn't mind at all if she showed up, too. The woman hesitated but went along, thinking the two reporters were friends. They were merely working acquaintances from different stations.

Ask yourself if this is how you would handle that situation. Maybe explaining to the victim that you'd like her story because it could help other potential victims realize the dangers might be a better route. You determine for yourself, and get views from other trusted people in your newsroom.

Finally, you need to garner respect, and there's no easier way to gain it than by being honest. When calling up victims, tell them honestly, "I'm sorry about what happened, but I wonder if I could talk to you about it on camera?" If they're upset by your call, respect them if they ask not to be called back. Or ask if later might be a better time. If you see that same person on another station's air, ask yourself if you weren't compassionate enough with them on the phone. Aim for the positive. If the person is upset with you on the phone say, "Don't hang up. We'd like to hear your story, and try to get the word out so that this doesn't happen to others. I understand that you're upset, and I don't look forward to calling people in this situation, but we hope we can help others." A lot of times the person will realize that you're just trying to do your job. Sometimes that bit of humane treatment and kindness will get you the interview when other reporters are getting the hang-up.

Or face it, sometimes people just won't talk to you because they don't watch your station or don't like your anchors. It's frustrating, but it does happen. Still, explaining that telling their story might help others may turn them around. If they're rude, don't be rude back. That way, they'll never change their minds about you or your station. And who knows, maybe sometime down the line, if there's a jury trial or another follow-up involved, your compassion will pay off.

Here's an example. A reporter in a small market was assigned to talk to a woman about her missing daughter. Forensics tests had determined that some remains found recently were those of the little girl. The woman had no telephone, so the only point of contact was face to face at her home. The reporter in this case went up to the front door alone, keeping the photographer in the car. A few words of "I'm sorry about your daughter, and for what your family must be going through. Would you mind telling me what she was like?" made the mother feel enough at ease to let in the reporter. She was able to compose herself enough, so that when she was ready, the reporter summoned the photographer and conducted the interview. If she'd opened the door to a reporter, photographer, news camera, and light kit, she might not have granted the interview. The fact that this reporter kept in mind that this woman was a person, a grieving mother, and not just an interview, probably made all the difference.

> "Always take the blame for your own mistakes. There is nothing worse than trying to palm off your mistakes on others. If you don't do something right, admit it, move on, and don't do it again."
>
> Hayley Herst, assignment manager

In the newsroom, be honest about your mistakes. Newsrooms are rife with rumors about who missed a story and why it was missed. Those rumors grow into legends very quickly. Make sure it's not about you. If you missed a story, tell people you did, and why. Maybe you were on the phone when the action was happening on the scanner, helping out someone else. If you're a technical person, admit you didn't punch up camera one instead of camera two, and the wrong anchor was on air. People will know you did it anyway, so just do two things. Own up to it, and resolve not to repeat the mistake. Then move on.

> TV news has the unique power to influence and impress. It's your job to take advantage of that without taking advantage.

8

ONE-MAN BANDS

You may have heard of one-man bands, but what are they? Easy. It's probably you on your first job, especially if you're working in a small or medium market. But large markets also use them.

Basically, a one-man band is a reporter, photographer, assignment editor, and videotape editor all in one. You. You'll think up the story, make the calls, set up the story, shoot the interview, conduct the interview, shoot your stand-up, write the story, and edit the story. Sometimes, you're even the anchor. This sounds like a lot of work. It is. It sounds like an ineffective way to get the best story. It is. It sounds like the cheapest way to get the story. It is. And it sounds like a great way to get a lot of experience. It is.

Why do stations use this format to get news? Money. It's a lot cheaper to have a few people with many skills, than a lot of people with few skills. In some stations, there are variations. Sometimes reporters trade off being the photographer for each other on stories. That saves money on a photographer.

"When I started out as a television news photographer, I didn't realize how much of a communicator you need to be. I didn't develop the reporting skills I needed in college. I thought the reporter would take care of that end. But I found I have to be the reporter, too."

Eric Kehe, photographer

PROS AND CONS

While it certainly is a lot of work being a one-man band, there is a definite upside. First and foremost, you have control over your story. You can't be frustrated with the photographer for not quite getting the shot you wanted. You got just the one you wanted. And you know exactly how it's all going to edit together. And since you shot the video and wrote to it, you know where everything is on tape, and can edit quickly.

Beyond all this, you are getting the best thing you can get: experience. You'll come out of this market knowing how to shoot, write, interview, and edit. Even if you never pick up a camera again in your career after this job, you will know just what it takes to be a photographer, reporter, writer, and editor. For reporters, it helps you write to video better, and learn how important it is to know what the lens is picking up. It can really add to your story. It also helps to learn how to interview. The first time you're on a tight deadline, and wading through twenty minutes of interview footage, you learn how to ask only questions you need and not waste time and tape.

For photographers, you really learn a sense of what you need to shoot to visually tell a good story. Things like natural sound, matched action, or making sure you hold your shots long enough and waiting until the subject has walked out of frame. (All things that will make it quicker and easier when it's time to edit.)

Editors learn from this experience what restrictions the photographer was working with at the time, and how the reporter wrote to the video.

All of these things, tough as they may be at the time, add up to good solid background and experience, whatever you want to do in the newsroom.

However, this experience comes at a price. The price of not creating the best stories you can. Face it, we all have strengths and weaknesses. Very few of us are good at shooting, writing, interviewing, and editing. Reporters will find it harder to shoot, to get good shots, and to deal with the technical side. The most common problem: forgetting to white-balance and coming back to the station with blue or yellow video. And those shots had to be used, even though they weren't professional quality. Many reporters who had to use those old 6-inch tube cameras learned a very important lesson. Don't shoot at a light source. A lot of old-timer reporters-turned-shooters made this faux pas: they went to a fire and shot the sun gleaming like an eerie orange ball behind the smoking ruins of the burning building. It's a great shot, until you get back to the station. The bright sun "burned" a hole into the tube, and every shot thereafter, for days after in fact, had a large blue circle in the corner, where the bright sun was. Also, you may not get audio during interviews, or may forget to use lights indoors, and so on. It's really very embarrassing asking the governor to give you a private SOT because you forgot to turn on the mic during his press conference.

Another downside is, you may miss something important while dealing with all the technical issues of the camera, lights, and audio, like the vote at a city council meeting, or an impromptu interview with a top city official who happens to be at the council meeting.

When you go to edit, you'll find you didn't get the shots you needed to piece the story together. And on and on. The same thing happens to photographers, producers, or editors. You may not have asked the right questions. You didn't check facts, and got part of a story wrong. These are all dangers of doing things you're not really set up to do.

GET FAMILIAR

You may be saying to yourself, well, now that I know about one-man bands, I won't go to a station that uses them. Stations may tell you that they don't use them, but there is hardly one out there that doesn't. In smaller markets, you may even be asked to submit something that you've shot and edited yourself. It may well be the difference between getting the job or losing it. So it's a good idea to familiarize yourself with the equipment and how it works.

The Betacam™ is the standard across-the-board camera for most stations. With the advent of digital technology, some larger stations are going to digital beta, which means the tape and editing equipment are in a digital format. However, the camera stays the same. It's

EQUIPMENT TABLE

Tape Formats for Newsrooms

Betacam™ (Oxide or SP)	Analog, uncompressed tape format.
BetaSX™	Digital, compressed tape format. Looks like a betacam tape.
DVCam™	Sony's version of digital compressed tape format. Smaller cassette.
DVCPro™	Panasonic's version digital compressed tape format. Looks like a DVCam.
MiniDV™	Consumer version of digital tape. Smaller tape format.
3/4" (U-Matic)™	3/4" tape format. Used to be the standard for newsrooms in the '70s and '80s. Big bulky video cassettes.
S-VHS™	Analog tape format. Looks like a VHS tape. An inexpensive format. Not used much anymore.

heavy, and not easy to handle for smaller women. They're also expensive and delicate pieces of equipment, so they need to be handled with care. An inexperienced person will most likely miss any spot news trying to get the camera turned on and up and running.

Other stations may use DV-cams or S-VHS. These will be much easier to handle, but they don't have the picture quality or the durability.

Don't worry. A major equipment failure will happen at the exact moment the jury announces the verdict, or during some incredible spot news. It's the inevitable Murphy's Law of news. You can avoid

"My biggest challenge initially was getting the job. There were no female TV news photographers in Arizona when I started. I was it. So management was skeptical that I could physically do the work. But once we all got past that I did fine, I was even the first female to win the `Best News Photographer' Emmy in Georgia."

Carol Lynde, photographer

some of the most common problems just by being conscientious. Here's a checklist.

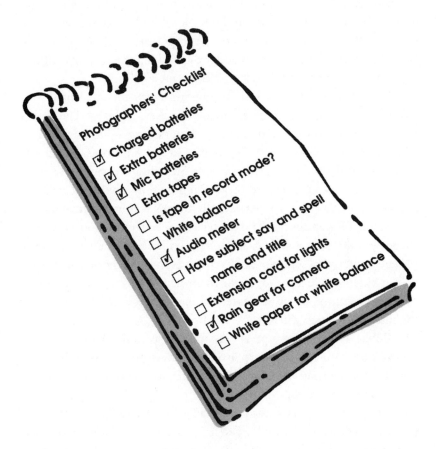

Probably the most common mistake is to not check the batteries. A battery will go dead at the crucial moment. Same thing with a microphone battery. You'll have video, but not audio. A pair of headsets allows you to check audio without disturbing the reporter and interviewee. Also, carry extra light bulbs, because a light can go out at any time. Make sure you carry an extra tape, just in case. Make sure the red record tab is pushed in, so you can record. If you press play and record and it doesn't record, this is probably the problem. Don't forget to white balance. Otherwise, you'll either have blue video or yellow video. And don't forget to turn on the mic. The simplest way to avoid that error is to check the audio meter when interviewing, or even when shooting b-roll. A good rule of thumb is to always ask the interviewee to say and spell his/her name on tape. It never fails. If the person's name is John Smith, and you don't bother to ask, his name will actually be spelled Jon Smythe. And get their title on tape too. Nothing will make someone madder than giving them an instant demotion (i.e., listing a president of a company as VP).

What happens if your school program never included hands-on training? Don't worry. There are many easy ways to learn. The best is to get an internship at a station, and just work with a photographer or editor to let them show you the ropes. Go out on shoots, pay attention to what the photographer is doing. Stay after the show, and see if someone will take the time to show you how things work. Have these people critique your work periodically to gauge your improvement.

Some TV stations don't take interns that aren't in school. If you've already graduated and need to learn, check into classes at a community college or technical school. Or there may even be a school that specializes in video production. Most of them have some type of television production course. If this isn't extensive enough, you may be able to get the internship, since you're back in school.

Public access TV is a great way to learn as well. Many public access stations want public participation and will have workshops on how to run the gear. Then you're on your own, and you can learn at your own pace, on your own time.

There really is no excuse for not acquiring these skills. In the long run, they will serve you well. Even if you start off at a large market station and never put them to use, you'll gain a deeper understanding of the jobs and people that make a newsroom run. More about how this will help you out later.

Remember, this is the information business, and it never hurts to know more.

Be a reporter, be a photographer, be an assignment editor, be a producer. Be all you can be.

9

THE STORY

Reporters, it will take you *forever* to complete your first few stories, no matter how simple they are. Blame it on nerves, blame it on learning the ropes, blame it on the photographer . . . you will be *slow!* Don't worry. It happens to everyone. It will take you hours to set up interviews, what seems like an eternity to shoot the story, and many stress-filled hours to log, write, and voice your package. And don't forget about the frustrations you'll face trying to edit under deadline pressure! You have two choices:

1) Struggle through and learn the hard way, or
2) Listen up to a few tips designed to rev up the storytelling engine in us all.

Producers, photographers, and assignment editors, don't go away. There's plenty for you to learn by reading this information, too.

WHO, WHAT, WHEN, WHERE, WHY, AND HOW?

Information. It's the fuel that feeds the television news machine. It is your mission, no matter what your job in the newsroom, to gather as much information as you possibly can about everything. Read newspapers and magazines, surf the net, listen to news radio, watch news shows, local and national, and international, too, and don't forget to

**Who? Where?
What?   When?
Why?   How?**

talk to people in your neighborhood, at the grocery store, at the gas station. Some of the best news stories come out of people talking about their own lines of specialty.

INFORMATION OVERLOAD

The tough part about information is how to filter and organize it. Sometimes you'll not have enough, but more often, you'll have way too much. Part of that is our fault. Most people who work in television news are copious note takers. We write down everything! While it is good to have lots of information, it's not so good to have so much that you can't possibly fit it into a 1:20 package. This is where the art of recognizing what's important comes into play. It's an acquired art, a skill that rarely comes naturally.

So, be prepared to work at it. Here's a real-life example that might help you remember to wade through those pages and pages of notes, press releases, statistics, and official statements for what's important to your viewers.

The final section of the beltway is about to open. It's been more than ten years in the making and finally, drivers will have a way to bypass downtown in forty minutes rather than the hour-plus commute through the heart of the city. There is a catch. The highway is a toll road. It will cost drivers eight dollars and fifty cents to take it, forty-seven miles, from one end to the other. The speed limit is seventy miles per hour. More than five million man-hours went into planning and construction. Workers poured more than 300 thousand cubic yards of concrete and built eighty-eight bridges during construction, The total cost of the project added up to more than 1.2 billion dollars. Drivers can expect to pay tolls for at least thirty years.

Wow! All that from one press release. (It's true; we didn't make this one up!) And that was just part of a long list of fun facts the PR person fired off to reporters, producers, and assignment desks across the city. The challenge was to pick and choose which stats meant the most to viewers and weave them into a news-you-can-use preview story without putting viewers to sleep. Take a minute right now and write down how you would handle this story. If you're a reporter or a photographer working on your own, who do you talk to out in the field? If you're a producer and have to look through the video and write it without being there, how will you do this?

Here's how two stations handled it.

The first station got shots of the construction, then interviewed drivers at a nearby gas station to ask if they would use the toll road. Many didn't want to pay the extra cost.

Here's the lead-in:

Anchor: "It's taken more than ten years and one-point-two billion dollars to build. The result? Forty-seven miles of highway, eighty-eight bridges, and three hundred thousand cubic feet of concrete. But with a toll of eight dollars and fifty cents, will drivers want to use it?"

Take Split (this is the double-box shot with the anchor on the left and the reporter on the right).

Anchor: "News 7's Felicia Martin is live at the brand new I-35 toll road now with more."

Felicia: "That's right, Ed. This may be the road to nowhere if no one wants to use it."

Take Package.

As a viewer, I don't think I want to hear more! That's too much information already, and the cutesy cliché in the toss doesn't help. I'm glazed over, and I change the channel, to News 3.

Anchor: "It's forty-seven miles long and more than ten years in the making. And, it opens tomorrow."

SS Map (this is a full-screen graphic of the toll road's route).

"The final stretch of the beltway will give drivers a shortcut around downtown traffic. But, News 3's Stan Stanfield says those drivers should keep two things in mind."

Take Split:

"He's live tonight at the new I-35 beltway interchange at Maple Avenue. Stan, what two things are you talking about?"

Stan Remote (Stan holds up a dollar bill and a pocket watch): "Money and time. Because this impressive-looking highway is all about spending one to save the other."

Take Package.

From there, the reporter went on to tell a story about how workers were putting the last-minute touches on a road that would save commuters time, but cost them money. There was video and sound of construction equipment moving that last pile of dirt, painters touching up highway signs, and technicians testing computerized tollbooths. The reporter broke down the miles and the minutes using an animated graphic of a car traveling the new road versus a straight shot through downtown at rush hour. There was also a graphic of the price tags of the toll costs. The package ended with one of the construction workers hopping into a street sweeper and heading off to brush the dust off the road. No information overload. Just enough. The story was told through the workers, with the statistics (money, time, and distance) that meant the most to drivers in the viewing audience. The rest of the myriad of facts and figures was saved for the newspaper.

How did the reporter achieve all this? First off, *WIIFM,* what's in it for me? (More on WIIFM in chapter 12.) Why does anyone care about a new road? Well, where will it take me, and why would I use it? And how much will it cost me? All three elements were contained in the package. The reporter set up a tollway tour. A simple call to the PR person and the crew was on its way to get visuals and sound. They donned hard hats and loaded up with a project planner. They shot construction workers putting the finishing touches on the road and tollbooths. They taped interviews with some of the workers and the project planner. They also made sure to record any and all natural sound, such as the sounds of construction equipment, the sound of wheels on the road, and so on. The idea was to give viewers something they couldn't see for themselves: an inside look at a superhighway before it opens.

Back at the station, the reporter logged the tape . . . not just the bites, but the nat sound too. He went to the graphics person and explained his graphics, the simple map of the toll road, the animated one of the car going around the beltway, and the price tags. From the start, the reporter had a clear *focus* on what the story was about. Without that focus, the story is all over the place, in fact it's not a *story* at all. Just a jumble of facts and figures viewers will never remember because they aren't given a reason to.

The first reporter never mentioned just how much time the road would save. She just mentioned the money factor. Of course she got negative bites . . . because she didn't explain the time savings to the people she talked to. She mentioned this information somewhere in the tag. Sometimes you have to look beyond the press release to come up with the news-you-can-use. If you don't give viewers the reason to watch the story in your lead, they most likely won't.

And the impetus isn't always on the reporter to come up with the great nugget of the story. A good assignment editor would have asked the PR person about the time factor. Many times they won't know, then they'll check it out and call you back. That way the reporter doesn't waste a lot of time sitting around the station waiting for a call back. The assignment editor already did the legwork for her. And producers, as you're in the assignment meeting, mention this to the reporter. Most stories are talked about in the meeting, with producers and managers discussing various angles. Producers also need to take it upon themselves to send reporters out on the street fully armed with the best information and ideas they can have. Teamwork is such a factor in every story.

REACH OUT AND TOUCH YOUR CONTACTS

Then there's the telephone and e-mail. Get used to talking, for hours, on the phone and typing until your fingers go numb. This is where

Call Every Week

- ☑ Contact in police detective dept.
- ☐ Contact in arson unit
- ☑ Contact in mayor's office
- ☐ Check with police on Internet fraud investigation
- ☑ Call Senator Brown's office on Immigration Bill
- ☑ Get update with Dept. of Transportation highway const...

Call Every Month

- ☐ Follow up on housing condemnation story
- ☑ Follow up on ski area accident
- ☐ Call attorney for shooting case
- ☑ Check with developer on mall construction story
- ☐ Call Council Clerk on progress on new jail site
- ☐ Check with health dept. on air pollution story

you put your Rolodex of contacts to use. Make up a couple of lists: those contacts you call regularly and those you call every once in a while. These are the folks who will keep you "tuned in" to the outside world. Then start making the calls and writing the e-mails, every day. This includes following up on stories you've done or assigned. Don't just forget about them. Most stories take months, sometimes years, to develop. It's your chance to shine when the media spotlight has faded and everyone else has forgotten about them.

Also, make sure you have a current copy of the phone book, both white and yellow pages. If you have specific questions about a specific issue or subject, call the contact who can help you. Even if you think this person may not be able to help directly, he or she may be able to point to even more contacts.

For instance, you need to find out if a guy arrested overnight for arson has bonded out of jail. The first call should be to the jail. If the staff there can't (or won't) help you, try the detectives at the police department, sheriff's office, or the arson unit of the fire department. See how having a contact can help? Even if they can't go "on record," they can give you a lot of leverage. Try the PIO at the fire department. If you learn that the suspect is out of jail, track him down. Arrest affidavits at the police department list home addresses (and these are public information). See if he'll talk. Will his neighbors talk? Many newsrooms subscribe to an Internet information service that will allow you to search motor vehicle, voter, and countless other databases for individual people. If you have it, use it.

DON'T BE SHY

Once you have the information you're looking for, set up an interview. This is TV, after all. You need that person who just told you everything over the phone or online to do the same on camera, right? This one's easy, just agree on a time and a place. If the person is reluctant to go on camera, try a trick we always use. They think the story is important enough to be aired on TV, right? Then it's their responsibility to follow through. And it's to their benefit to have their side told by an actual person, not just the reporter. It's a lot more powerful and will really hit home. Usually this argument can persuade many of those willing to tell you the story, but not on camera.

Now, start thinking about what video you'll need to illustrate the story. Going back to our arson story. No one from your station was sent to shoot the fire . . . it didn't sound big enough on the scanner. What do you do? Get creative. Get morning-after video of the burned-out building. Maybe there are some neighbors around who witnessed the fire. If so, knock out an interview. Maybe a neighbor saw someone shooting the fire with his camcorder. Track that person down, and *bingo,* you have exclusive video. Either way, don't leave until you get the neighbor's phone number, e-mail address, or some way to get back in touch with that person.

When you're conducting the interview, don't stress over what questions to ask. It's easy to get so worked up about asking all the questions you'll need to get all the information, and then forget the most important one. Always make sure to cover the basic who, what, when, where, how, and why. But, some of the best soundbites pop out when you're simply talking to whoever you're interviewing. Discuss what you're there to find out instead of interrogating. And *listen.* Sometimes the best questions on your part come in a follow-up to what the interviewee just said. Or, if you like what the person said, but they didn't say it concisely, re-ask the question in a different way. You can say something like, "so what you're saying is. . . ."

Remember, you're a reporter on a news story, not someone making commercials from a preset script. Don't ask someone to re-state what they just told you, and never put your words in their mouths. We've heard reporters say, "say that again, just say it this way." That's not the way to conduct an interview. Your job as a writer is to structure your writing around what your soundbites say. And your job as a reporter is to ask the right questions in the right way so you can write around your soundbites. It's challenging, and sometimes tricky, but mastering these skills is what makes a good and solid writer and reporter. You're not just writing the story, you're also reporting it, as it was told to you. If you come back to the station, and the soundbites only say "yes" and "no," you know to ask more open-ended questions, like "what did you see?" instead of "did you see anything suspicious?"

Okay, photographers, assignment editors, and producers, here's where you come in.

Photographers, when you're out with reporters, and the reporter wraps up the interview without asking a certain question, jump right in and ask. We have always been grateful to photographers who did this. Instead of being upset that they were overstepping their bounds, it was great to have an extra pair of ears listening to what was going on. Sometimes, as a reporter, you're formulating that next question, or writing in your notebook, instead of really listening. The photographer may be listening for you, and may ask that follow-up question that will give you that great bite you may have missed. Many times these were the gold nuggets that really *tell* the story.

Assignment editors, you'll be asking the questions all day long, over the phone. Many times, you're the first contact anyone at the station will have with the subject. You'll really be the gatekeeper to decide if the story is worth doing. If you don't do this, you could miss a worthwhile story. Again, finding out the motive is all-important here. You don't want to send your crew out on stories that sound great over the phone but then don't pan out when you find out the other side.

Producers, you'll set up stories too, set up field shoots for crews, and maybe, if you're lucky, go out on shoots yourself. You'll need those interviewing skills on a daily basis, and those writing skills.

PRODUCING THE STORY

Live by this mantra. Don't just write . . . produce your story. That's right, produce. A television news story isn't just video and sound tied together by your words. It's the whole package. Think about what video and sound is most compelling. Will graphics or animation help or hinder the story you're crafting? And, how can you best use the live shot to tie it all together?

VIDEO AND SOUND

Work closely with the photographer on this one. Discuss the best way to visualize the story . . . before, during, and after you've finished shooting. During an interview, listen and take note of the best sound-bites. See if there are any natural sound opportunities that the re-porter can write into the story, sound like rushing water, traffic, barking dog, crying baby, ringing phone, and so on. These are things that really bring your story to life.

GET CREATIVE

There's nothing that says your story with all the facts and figures can't also be a work of art. Let your creative juices flow. When you're un-der severe deadline pressure, of course, is not the time to sit and con-template the universe. But when you have the extra time, do it. And sooner or later, you'll develop a sixth sense for seeing the same old story in a different way.

Take the time a reporter was assigned to cover the opening day of a rodeo. The rodeo was a big deal in a midsized town; plus, the station had sponsored this event for years. A new assignment editor was determined to cover his end, and make sure nothing was missed. He sent a crew to cover the opening of the rodeo at 6 A.M.! Needless to say, nothing was going on. No one was around. Well, almost. Most reporters would have called the desk and chewed out the assignment editor for being so stupid. Not this reporter. He found the one person who was at the fairgrounds, and got his story. It happened to be an old man who cleaned the horse stalls, and had done so for years. He was proud to help out the cowboys, and he knew everything there was to know about the competitors and their horses. This reporter came back with an unforgettable story from this old hand's point of view. And just for fun, he threw in a lighthearted little point of view from the horses' standpoint. This guy made their lives a lot more comfortable, and here was someone who knew all their quirks and habits. How many people would come away from that situation with a potential Emmy award–winning story on their hands? Looking at the world in just a slightly different way could make you one of them. Herein lies the difference between an everyday reporter, and someone who really touches their viewers.

A little bit later we talk about finding the nugget in everyday people, that just about anyone has a story to tell. Consider yourself the key that unlocks those treasures. It's not going to happen every day, but these stories are the reason why many people get into the business, and why they stay in. These are the stories that colleagues and viewers just won't forget.

TALK IT OUT

You probably already know this one: Write like you talk. It's a no-brainer, right? Possibly the one most distinctive mark of a beginning writer is writing like a newspaper reporter. And that leads to awkward sentences that aren't easy to read out loud. If you're really having trouble, the best way to handle the writing is to sit back and just start talking out loud, to your best friend, your spouse, significant other, parent, or whoever you imagine is waiting to hear what's going on.

That way you eliminate for good the "authorities say," and the "suspect fled from the scene and is still at large." Would you ever say that in real life? Then don't on the air, either. Also, if you're an on-air talent, nothing will help you get more comfortable talking to a camera than easy-to-read, conversational writing.

The reporter is *not* the story. You make the story come alive, but resist the temptation and keep yourself out of it. One of the worst examples: a news reporter who asked herself the question: What would I do if I won the lottery? The answer: Who cares!

THE STAND-UP

A reporter stand-up in a package can do one of two things. It can move the story forward or it can stop it, cold. Work to make your stand-ups memorable, not mundane. Strive to incorporate some sort of action or movement. If the story is about an automobile recall because of faulty brakes, use a car in your stand-up. But, don't just stand in front of it spouting facts and figures. Walk up to the wheel well, kneel down, and point out what the recall is all about. A little imagination goes a long way. But, remember, not every story needs a stand-up. Trust your instincts. If it doesn't feel right, don't do it.

BRING IT ALIVE, WITH LIVE

Many reporters and producers believe it best to tell the entire story in the package. We agree, to a point. Packages need to be able to stand alone. In other words, they need to tell the complete story without the benefit of a live shot or complicated anchor setup. But, there's nothing like a motivated, show-and-tell live shot to grab the viewers' attention and keep it hooked. Think of it like a rocket launching the space shuttle. Without the blast-off, it's just not that interesting. Add fire to your packages through your live shots. Here are a couple of ideas:

1. The story was about a deer leaping a low spot in a fence next to the interstate, running into traffic, and causing a deadly car wreck. The reporter on this story actually hopped the fence in the live shot to demonstrate how easy it was to do.
2. The story was about a new Internet website where you can sign up on a list to keep telemarketers from calling you at home. The reporter on this story went live with a computer as a prop and showed how quick and easy it was to sign up online.
3. Or this one. The story was about park rangers chasing a bear through a neighborhood and finally trapping and sedating it in a neighbor's backyard. The reporter on this story went live from the spot, just yards away from a child's swing set, where the rangers successfully snared the bear.

The point of all these live shot ideas is that a picture can tell a thousand words. And action will get a reaction. Why struggle to *tell* how close to homes the bear is, when you can *show* it all? Chances are, viewers won't miss that point.

THE FULL STORY

Now that you have the pieces, it's time to put them together. The best television news stories *flow*. They have a definite beginning, middle, and end. So, work to make each piece fit into the next. Start with the anchor intro to set up the live shot. Then blast off with the active live shot straight into the package. And, finally, tie it all together with a brief, live tag.

The worst thing you can do is to write your package first. Reporters who do this either:

A) Repeat themselves in the intro and tag . . . or,
B) Waste valuable time trying to take out information from the package and rewrite it as a lead-in and tag.

That's because all their information is in the package and there's nowhere to go from there. Start from the beginning and end with the ending. Write your lead-in first, then your package, then your tag. Easy and simple.

WATCH OUT FOR:

Wordy intros and tags
Facts and figures
Anchor questions

WATCH OUT FOR . . .

- Wordy intros and tags: Keep them brief. Get to the point. 10–15 second intro, 10–15 second live toss to package, 10–15 second live tag.
- Facts and figures: If you have to use them, make them understandable. Simple graphics are often the best way to do this. Don't just repeat back what the press release said. If the numbers don't make any sense to you, they won't to your viewers, either.
- Anchor questions: Suggest a few questions, in advance, that the anchors may want to ask rather than being blindsided on air.

AND REMEMBER

Work with, not against, your co-workers. Any story requires many hands to shape it for air. Reporters, photographers, assignment editors, producers, and video editors are all on the same team. It may not always seem like it, but they are. Talk to each other. Brainstorm on how best to tell the story with the elements you have, including video, sound, information, and live shot opportunities. Reporters, timecode specific video and sound on the package script. This will make it much easier and ultimately faster for photographers and editors to put together the finished product. Photographers and editors, if you have an idea to improve the story, like adding a soundbite or re-shooting a stand-up . . . tell the reporter. More times than not, they'll thank you. And, when that creatively shot, well written, and superbly edited story hits the air, you'll all know that you did your best to make it the best.

Do it right the first time. You have no second chances to tell the story.

10

WHERE TO GO, WHAT TO DO, WHO TO CALL?

We talked earlier about the PIO, the public information officer. Much of your job will depend on your relationship with these all-important information gatekeepers. The key word is *relationship*. That means lots of phone calls and e-mails on a regular basis—not just when you need information for a story. Some PIOs are highly accessible and media-friendly, others are not. Some will return your calls and be willing to chat it up, while others will react as though you're wasting their time. It's a balancing act that you need to constantly work at perfecting. Once you have done so, you'll be the one getting the exclusive information and the stories that no one else has.

> "A good PIO quickly learns the needs of the media and knows how to get the media what they want. A good reporter should learn the same about the PIO! Go to lunch with your PIO. Call them just to say hello. Build trust . . . prove you can be trusted . . . and reap the rewards."
>
> Jacki Tallman,
> Sheriff's Department, PIO

THE OFFICIALS

This chapter is designed to help you wade through the seemingly endless list of "officials" you'll encounter reporting, producing, even researching a story. Some of them will turn out to be helpful and friendly. Others will turn on you. Pay close attention. Here we go.

THE COURTS

In the United States, court systems vary by state. So, where you are and how they work with media will largely dictate what you are able to report from court. You will find that some judges will allow cameras in the courtroom, while others won't. There is no rhyme or reason. In some states and cities you may have to file paperwork to get a camera in a high-profile murder trial. In others, the courts may contact the station with all the coverage details. The key is to know how your court system works. To find out, you have to ask.

Usually, the senior assignment editor at the station knows everything about the local court news coverage requirements. If not, ask the reporter who's been there the longest. And, if all else fails, pick up the phone and call the clerk of court.

For quick information out in the field make sure you know how to find the courthouse. And, more important, know how to find the clerk of court's office. You'll need to visit often for arrest affidavits, search warrant affidavits, and case filings. It's like a crime and justice library. The clerk is really the gateway to a lot of information. She/he will know which cases are going on, which have been postponed, which case is before which judge, and so on. Treat this person well!

The biggest mistake any reporter, producer, photographer, or assignment editor can make when it comes to court coverage is *not* taking the time to doublecheck facts. Take the case of the reporter covering the trial of a man accused of sexual assault on a child. And, keep in mind the whole "innocent until proven guilty" thing. In the live shot, the reporter mentioned something about the defendant having done this before. What he didn't say is that he overheard someone outside the court saying this. The reporter never bothered to check the defendant's police record. It turned out to be false information and the reporter nearly lost his job over it. Your words carry power. What if some of the jurors had gone home and seen that coverage? Sometimes they are instructed not to listen to or watch coverage of the case, but not always. You don't want to be the reason for a mistrial.

Here are some of the documents that would most likely be public record in most states, unless they are sealed by court order. Keep in mind, these documents can vary from state to state.

Local Law Enforcement Records
- Arrest Log (list of arrestees)
- Warrantless arrest affidavit
- Custody report
- Incident report (unless state law protects it, such as a child abuse report in some states)

Court Records
- Search warrant affidavit
- Search warrant return (what was found during a search)
- Arrest warrant affidavit
- Charging document (also called Complaint & Information)
- Minute Orders (also called Register of Actions)
- Grand Jury Indictment
- Criminal Summons and Complaint

Source: Lynn Kimbrough, PIO, City of Denver

THE COP SHOP

This one is relatively easy regardless of where you live and work. The two most important things you need to know are:

1) The name and phone number for the police public information officer or PIO and the district attorney, and
2) The location of the office where they file the police reports.

The police PIO and the district attorney can be the best contacts a newsroom can have. That is, *if* the people working in the newsroom have forged good relationships with them. No matter what your specific job, do yourself a favor and get on their good side. Take them out to lunch once in a while. Call them each day. Drop by their office once in a while to just talk. Chances are, after they get to know you they'll trust you and, ideally, call you with great stories. Develop relationships with officers and detectives, too. They are the ones with the real scoop.

Police reports are public record and, sometimes, the source of great stories. That's why it never hurts to go down to the police station and spend some time (when you have it) sifting through the piles of reports. It may sound like a needle in a haystack sort of thing. But, the first time you find that needle, it's all worth it.

LOCAL GOVERNMENT

For most cities, the mayor and city council make the big decisions. Consequently, they often spark the biggest controversies. The problem is, most of what they do isn't exactly lead story material. That's why it's important to sift through the boring stuff and find the stories people care about.

Step one, know your leaders. Remember the Rolodex? The mayor and council members' names and numbers should be in there. Also, know who the clerk of council is and how to contact him or her. The clerk is the one who handles all the dirty work for the council members. The clerk of council knows about the issues and who to contact for the best information. The clerk can also help you understand how local government works.

Step two, listen and learn. Before you attend that first city council meeting, check in with the clerk of council. Ask for a copy of the meeting agenda and ask the clerk to decipher it for you. Just how does a proposed ordinance become an ordinance? After the first reading, public comment, or after the second reading and full council vote? Knowing the details will help you navigate through the tedious red tape that is local government in action. And help you avoid some embarrassing mistakes.

STATE GOVERNMENT

Like city government, get to know the big players, from the governor on down. Most governors have a public information officer on staff. Immediately file that person's name and numbers in your Rolodex as well as those of as many legislators and legislative assistants as possible. The assistants and aides will be your best sources of information. And, they will be your best shot at getting a last-minute interview with the senator or representative. Make nice and smile.

For more information on all state offices and leaders go online. All states have their own websites that outline state government. Most feature bios on state leaders and updated outlines of pending legislation. There's a lot you can learn with the click of a mouse.

It's also good to know how a bill becomes a law. That way you won't get caught by surprise or feel like a fool down at the statehouse. Brush up.

And again, there's usually a clerk of each party who is in the know about many of the things you might need to know. Like, which hearings are going on today? Did the subcommittee meet on this issue yet? And so on. You don't need to be running all over the capitol building tracking down this information. Go straight to the source.

HOSPITALS

Not too complicated. Again, the PIO is the person to get to know. Many cities and counties have a number of different hospitals. So, check into them all. (Well, don't check in. Check them out!) Ask the PIO about the best way to get information on patients. How about weekends and after hours? Follow their rules and you'll be surprised at how helpful they can be . . . especially when you need information or an interview with a doctor in a hurry.

For reporters on-scene who need to know which hospital injured people are headed for, ask police officers first. If they don't know, call police and fire dispatch. Then call the hospital for a patient update.

Find out in advance what the rules are for getting the dramatic shots of the medical helicopter landing at the hospital. Most medical

> "Get what you need, then talk about something else for a couple of minutes. Be interested in the agency and the PIO."
>
> Jacki Tallman,
> Sheriff's Department, PIO

centers with helipads have specific spots from which television cameras are allowed to shoot. Same goes for the entrance to the emergency room. You don't want to be a photographer caught driving around the hospital not knowing this information.

WHAT YOU CAN AND CAN'T SAY, SHOOT, USE, OR BORROW, AND WHY

You may think you can say or shoot anything you want, and air anything you shoot. But, you'd be wrong. News operations are rife with lawsuits from viewers, companies, and just about anyone who feels a news crew violated their privacy or copyright or misrepresented them while putting together a story. Most stations have their own team of attorneys that helps make broadcast decisions for the newsroom. And, most hold legal seminars to help the news staff understand the ins and outs of broadcast law. Regardless, here are some general guidelines that we hope will help you make crucial decisions about your stories before airtime.

VIDEO AND HIDDEN CAMERAS

Reporters and photographers, this will happen to you. You're on the scene of breaking news. Let's say a gunman is holed up in a home across the street from a daycare center. The photographer shoots the scene from behind the police line. Police cars and officers are lining the street. Bystanders are watching from a distance. Concerned parents are rushing to pick up their children from the daycare. All of a sudden a neighbor runs up, shouting, "Get out of here. You can't shoot this.

Move or I'll have you arrested." Plain and simple, you're on a public street, behind police lines, shooting what everyone else can see with the naked eye. That neighbor is wrong. You can keep on doing what you're there to do because you're doing it in a public place. Now, if you were standing in their yard without their permission, they'd have a point.

Using hidden cameras is a bit more complicated. Generally, you can use them just about anywhere and be, legally, okay. But there are some exceptions. Say you're conducting an undercover investigation of alleged health violations at a local restaurant. You can take the camera into public areas of the restaurant that regular customers frequent. But, unless you recruit an employee to secretly tape for you, we'd advise that you stay out of the kitchen. Why? Because an attorney could argue in court that a restaurant kitchen is an employee-only area, off limits to customers. If the judge buys it, no matter how great the video, you and your station lose. The same goes for just about any business, school, agency, or office. And, of course, using a hidden camera on private property is out of the question, unless a co-owner or family member gives permission.

SOUND

When it comes to interviews, it's not so tricky. People will say either yes or no. But, what if you're knocking on doors with a stick mic in your hand and the camera following you, rolling tape? You ring the doorbell. A woman answers. You identify yourself, ask her a question, and she answers. Your story airs. The woman then calls the station and threatens to sue because she says she had no idea she was being taped. Legally, you should be okay. Why? Because it can be argued that the camera and microphone are an obvious tip-off. Still, it's always a good idea to ask before you roll tape.

The same goes when interviewing children. Most parents love to see their kids on television . . . unless it's in the context of something controversial or tragic. Here's an example. A news crew was sent to a high school to get students' reaction about their classmate who had suddenly dropped dead on the soccer field. It was easy enough to stop students as they left school. The reporter and photographer got emotional and touching interviews. The trouble came later, when their parents began to call the station demanding that their children not appear in the story. Some even threatened to sue. But, in the end, the station used the student interviews. Legally, they were covered. The crew had set up off school property, on a public sidewalk, and waited for the bell to ring. Some parents called back and apologized for overreacting after they saw the story. But others continued their protest because they felt the news crew should have asked their permission first. Bottom line, ask yourself one question: will this child's soundbite make or break the story, especially if you can't track down their parents before deadline? Then make a responsible decision. Especially if the story involves some kind of rumors about a school kid. You don't want to be sued by angry parents of a child other kids had said was mixed up in drugs or a gang. Many times the kids are right; many times they're just repeating rumors that have no foundation. Use a level head and good judgment in these cases. Are all the kids saying the same thing? Take the tape back to your station and get others' opinions, too. The last thing you want is to find out that some kids are saying things to the TV cameras because they don't like a particular kid and it's their fifteen minutes of fame. And always ask if they personally know the student, too. A lot of times you'll get blank looks, or they'll tell you the student in question is in their friend's gym class, but they don't really know that person at all.

PHONERS

Phone conversations work well in a pinch. You most often see them used in breaking news situations when a reporter has just arrived on-scene but a live truck isn't set up yet. Or they're used in interview situations with PIOs when a crew hasn't arrived on the scene. Example: an anchor talking with a search and rescue person for the latest developments in a small plane crash that happened in a remote area. Either a crew hasn't gotten there yet, or just can't get there.

Once in a while, though, you may have to tape a phone interview for a regular news story or an undercover investigative piece. When that happens it's important to know the legal dos and don'ts of taping telephone conversations.

Both federal and state statutes regulate electronic eavesdropping, including tape-recording conversations, and they are among the most important and confusing privacy laws affecting journalists. On the federal level, the law is generally considered a "one-party-consent" statute. That is, if one party to the conversation (e.g., the reporter) says it's okay to tape it . . . then it's okay, even if the person on the other end of the phone has no idea they're being recorded. On the state level things get a bit more jumbled. At least a dozen states require "two-party consent" when tape-recording conversations. That means both the reporter and the person he's interviewing must know and give permission before anyone presses the record button. There's even one state, Missouri, that is a one-party consent state except when it comes to using wireless microphones. Go wireless in the Show-Me state and you'll need two-party consent to tape an interview.

Laws change. That's why it's important to know where your state stands. Once you arrive at a new job in a new city, make a few calls to the local district attorney or the state attorney general's office. Ask them about privacy laws specific to that state. Check the web, too. Websites like www.spyman.com/laws list the states and where they stand regarding one- and two-party tape-recording laws.

Regardless, it's always best to let the person on the other end of the line know that what they say may end up on-air. If they protest, don't use it.

Attribute, attribute, attribute

Never convict someone on air! Always say "police say Joe Blow killed her then hid her body." Even "allegedly" won't get you off legally, so to be safe, attribute all your information to a police agency, court documents, or other sources.

DID I JUST SAY THAT?

Whether you're on-air or writing for the newscast, remember one thing. Words have power. And, depending on how you use them, you'll either get a pat on the back for telling a good story or a subpoena to appear in court.

The latter usually happens when someone appearing in or interviewed for a story feels that they were inaccurately depicted or that what they said was taken out of context. So choose your words carefully. Shy away from words like *allegedly* and *apparently*. Without verifiable facts, these words can be interpreted as misleading and even damaging in the context of a story. Consider this example. A news anchor reads the following script over video of police leading a man away in handcuffs. "Police lead Bill Smith, the alleged sexual predator, out of court after his preliminary hearing." First of all, who uses the word *alleged* in everyday conversation? (See chapter 12 for more on this.) And second, what if there is a mistake, and Bill Smith is released? He could come back and sue the station over the story in which he was labeled an "alleged sexual predator." Why? Because the person who wrote the story failed to attribute. They should have written something like this instead: "Police lead Bill Smith, the man investigators say is a sexual predator, out of court after his preliminary hearing."

Protect yourself and your station. Lose words like *alleged, allegedly, apparent,* and *apparently.* Chances are you'll stay out of court and write better, more accurate stories to boot. (More on this in chapter 12.)

STICK WITH THE OLD STANDBY

Claim is another word to shy away from. When you hear, "Ann Smith claims she was the victim of a kidnapping plot," what comes to mind? It sounds like the anchor doesn't believe Ann's story. It's not our job to cast these aspersions . . . that's for the police. Stick with the old standby, and you'll sound much more objective. "Police say Ann Smith told them a man grabbed her in a parking lot and tried to force her in the car. They're still looking for the car and its driver tonight." If police determine the case was a hoax, they'll let you know.

MUSIC AND MOVIE CLIPS

You may want to use music and movie clips to spice up your story from time to time. But, before you do, know one thing. It's not enough anymore to credit an artist, recording company, or movie studio. They want money for their material and they don't want you using it without paying up. This is not to say that you can't use clips under any circumstances. Just do a little research, first. When it comes to music, many stations have agreements with music licensing companies, agreements that allow you to use small bits of their music without penalty. Find out if your station has such an agreement before you press edit. As for movie clips, try not to use them unless you can get them off satellite feeds or promotional trailers. The days of renting a video or DVD at the video store and using what you want are over. People are watching—people who work for entertainment companies. And they will take your station to task if something they own is used improperly.

Stations who don't subscribe to these licensing fees have to be very careful. Even background music, at a bar for instance, could be called into question.

HERE'S THE SITUATION

You're sent to the state capitol to cover a (boring!) subcommittee meeting on a public transportation bill. Easy enough, you have the previous stories in your hand plus a few newspaper articles; all the info you'll need. Now you just need to pay attention to the meeting (yawn!), get a few bites, and most likely do a VO/SOT/SOT. No great shakes.

Your pager goes off. It's the desk, telling you that House Bill 487 was just passed . . . the assignment editor heard it on the radio as he was driving in to work that afternoon. Now you have two stories. You have to do the transportation VO/SOT/SOT *and* start getting a package together on HB487. Do all this in just a few hours. You call and ask the desk what HB487 is, and he says, "It's the public housing thing we've been following for weeks! Don't you know?" You hang up the phone and realize you should have been reading the paper a lot more closely. You have no idea what the "public housing thing" is. Time is ticking. What do you do? Your desk isn't much help right now, and you have no access to the Internet or a newspaper.

For starters, tell your photographer to keep listening in on what's going on in public transportation. If she hears anything good, tell her to note the timecode. Then go to the clerk of one of the parties, and ask that person about the bill. They'll give you some information. Next, ask who the sponsors are, and where their offices are located. Head on over. Talk to the folks in the sponsors' offices, then find out if you can set up an interview. Do you know what the legislators look like if you have to wait outside the legislative chambers? Usually, there's a picture of that person on the wall in their offices. Take a look. Find out what the representative's schedule is. That gives you some idea whether you should pull your photographer from the other meeting or let her hang out. Talking to the representatives' staffs should really help. And next time, keep up with what's going on, so you don't have to scramble.

In this situation, the reporter didn't get much help from the station. As an assignment editor, it's imperative that you not only know just about everything that's going on, make sure you share that information. If you're too busy at the moment, but you sense your field crew needs help, point them in the right direction. "I'm really busy, but head over to the GOP clerk's office. I told Sally you were coming, and she's getting together some information for you on HB487." That kind of direction could save the field crew a lot of precious time running around. Even if you are frustrated and feel that the reporter needs to brush up, your station's integrity is on the line. Helping out never hurts.

And the photographer is pivotal in this case. She's flying solo while the reporter is chasing down story number two. If *she* can't figure out which bites she's supposed to be listening for, the reporter is really in a bind. The station is expecting a VO/SOT/SOT and a package, and now you are under a lot of pressure, too. You'll need to listen carefully, note down the good bites, then edit them together when the live truck gets to the capitol.

We can't emphasize it enough—teamwork is the key to a solid news outlet.

Count on it. Official information will be released late in the day. Expect this, and stay ahead of the game.

11

MAKING DEADLINES

This should be a given. There is no alternative to missing a deadline. And bottom line, there is no excuse. There will be times (more than you'll care to think about), when you just don't think you're going to make it. Equipment will inevitably fail at a crucial moment, press conferences will be called right before news time, and that triple shooting at the convenience store will happen then, too. But despite all these things, there is no excuse to miss your news "slot." And these things will generally be the lead, because they're the most important and the most pressing. This will be one of the most difficult times, but it will separate the consummate professionals from the average Joe Newsperson.

The main thing is, don't panic. There are things you can do to better your odds at beating the clock and still put together a great story. We'll show you some pointers on how to do this, and how to never, ever miss your slot.

LEARN THE SYSTEM

For starters, learn the computer system. The last thing you need is to have a great story but miss your slot because you couldn't figure out how to save your story on the computer and you had to retype it. Since even the smallest news markets are becoming computerized, you'll need to know how to operate the system in a snap. Come in early or stay late, just typing dummy scripts.

Learn more than just how to type a package, if you're a reporter. What if you're asked to write an emergency VO or VO/SOT to help out the producer, or even during the show in the event of breaking news? Look at the script formats for each type of story. Even if you interned at a station and are familiar with their format, you're one step ahead, but each station does have its quirks. Some stations call the font "font," others call it "cg," or "chyron," still others call it "super." Make sure you know how your station designates things like this, and how the scripts should look. Make sure you know these things well enough so they don't slow you down when you're up against a deadline. Print out VO, VO/SOT, and package scripts as templates, so you can refer to them while you're typing. Learn how to save your scripts, and save them often . . . there's nothing worse than a power surge when you get up to check your video, and you come back to find your entire script is gone.

The same thing goes if you're a producer or an assignment editor. Producers work on the computer more than any other position in the newsroom. You're manipulating the rundown constantly, adding stories, deleting others, and moving some around to keep the newscast running smoothly. Know your rundown, and again, know how your station designates things like a double-box shot for live shots (2-box, box shot, side-by-side). There are many different terms for the same thing, so learn quickly how they do things where you are. Manipulate a rundown on your off-hours so you're able to do this when your back is up against the wall. Remember, the entire show is centered on the rundown, and the producer who's in control of it, so if you're not in control, the show is going down the tubes long before it hits air.

KNOW WHAT THEY WANT, WHEN THEY WANT IT

This is key. News operations have their own personalities. And, the people putting the show together have their own different likes and dislikes about how soon they want to see things like tease video and sound and stories. How soon should the live shot be tuned in? Will someone be around to record the package when the field crew is ready to feed it in? Reporters, ask the producer to let you know what she needs and when. And, talk to the station engineers about how to contact them when the time comes to feed tape from the field. Producers, tell the reporters what you need and when and keep in contact with the station engineers about tape feeding in from the field. And, assignment editors, stick your noses in everyone's business to make sure it happens.

Don't get bogged down. *KISS* or *keep it simple, stupid!* You'll be amazed at how often you'll have to remind yourself of this one, but it really works.

When you write your story, especially when you're under severe deadline pressure, *keep it simple!* This isn't the time to worry about an Emmy. Just get it done . . . that is your number one priority. The number one problem beginning writers have is not being able to separate out the essential facts. Remember, time is of the essence. A newspaper doesn't have the time or space restrictions that you have. A newscast, on the other hand, has to give viewers as many relevant stories as possible in only a few minutes. So, if your story is too long, the producer will have to drop other stories that viewers may have been interested in. Keep that in mind. Let the paper give every single detail. You concentrate on keeping it simple, yet informative, no easy task.

ORDER OF IMPORTANCE

Under deadline, include only the most important information in your story. Avoid getting caught up in the superfluous. For instance, when you're at the scene of breaking news like a major pile-up on the interstate . . . find out and report:

1) What happened?
2) Why?

3) Witnesses?
4) How many people injured or killed?
5) How many cars involved?
6) How long before the road is opened to traffic?
7) Alternate routes?

Don't worry about things like the ratio of cars to trucks, or the exact mile marker. Stick to finding the answers to questions you would want answered if you drove up on the wreck.

WRITING ON THE FLY

You just finished your last interview one hour before show time. The clock is ticking. Write on the fly. Let the photographer drive while you log sound and video in the camera and write your story on the way back to the station or on the way to the live shot. This is a great time saver and a sure-fire deadline beater.

TIMECODE

The single most important thing any reporter, producer, or writer can do to speed the editing process is to log the timecode of every piece of video and sound that they will write to in a story. There isn't always time to do it for every story, but when you can . . . *do!* A time-code on a script will allow the editor to immediately find it on the raw tape. There is no wasted time searching for the shot or sound bite they think you want.

LEARN WHAT'S EXPECTED OF YOU

For starters, when you know time is short, start thinking and planning ahead. You should be doing this anyway, every time, because you'll never know what will happen. Here's an example. You are covering a court case that's especially grisly: a wife has murdered her husband with an ax. Today's testimony promises to be compelling: the teenaged children are set to testify about their father's abuse of their mother. It's only a half-day of court, because the judge has something else to attend to. You're on your way back to the station when there's a bank robbery in progress. You're about a block away. This could be a live shot at 5, or it may be nothing. The station asks you to check it out. Here's your dilemma. The court story was very compelling, and could be a lead. You've got tons of great bites. But this bank robbery incident could be important. Are there customers or tellers at risk? Is anyone taken hostage? Is this the same guy who's been terrorizing local banks over the past year or so? Or, is this a false alarm? Either way, time is ticking, your story still has to be on the 5 P.M. newscast, and you're the only crew who could potentially get some great video of this robbery in progress.

It turns out that the guy is already gone, police are conducting a house-to-house search, and the nearby elementary school is on lockdown. You get video of police conducting the search, bites with neighbors, and some parents who've heard the news on the radio and have come to pick up their kids. The assignment desk has found out that this *is* the guy who's robbed several banks before, and they ask you to stay out there at the scene. This could potentially be a live shot lead for 5, with the court story as second. However, you have all the tapes, five twenty-minute tapes, and it's too late for someone from the station to drive all the way to the scene, pick them up, take them back, and have someone else look through them. How are you going to handle all this?

Thank your lucky stars you were on the ball during court proceedings. You glanced at the clock every time you heard a good bite of testimony. You know each tape is twenty minutes long. The photographer has marked each one in order. If court started at 9:00, and you heard some really great testimony at 10:15, where do you check? Tape 4, about fifteen minutes in. Simple. And, if you had been sitting next to the photographer, you could have made it even easier. Just glance over and check the timecode on the camera. It's synched up with the timecode on the tape. That way you don't need to shuttle through miles of testimony to write your story. Also, while you're sitting in court, *listen*. This is the strongest tool you have. Now you can start structuring your story even before you leave the courtroom.

You'll have a good idea of the story already. Observe reactions from key players in the case, the defendant, the victim or her family, and so on. The other smartest thing you can do is familiarize yourself with the case. Usually there's a file in the newsroom, kept by the assignment desk. You don't want to waste time wondering what's going on, or who each witness is, while you're in court. Don't sit and wonder about the significance of a kitchen knife when you know the victim was hacked to death with an ax. If you'd read the newspaper articles saved in the file, you'd know that a knife found at the scene is believed to have belonged to the murderer. And so on. You'll immediately know what's going on and won't spend time wondering.

It's hard enough sometimes to stay awake in court. Every tiny detail must be presented, must be wrapped up, cleared up. It's tedious, even for an exciting court case. There is hardly ever anyone shouting that someone in the audience is the guilty one, or slamming his fist on the witness stand, like TV dramas.

In reality, courtroom drama *isn't*. So, knowing what's going on, and why an attorney is asking a line of boring questions, will help you know where he or she is leading. You can spend this time, instead of sleeping or thinking about what your after-work plans are, by writing the story in your head, or in your notebook. That way, when you leave the courtroom, your story is practically written . . . just drop in the bites, and the editor is ready to go. And you are ready to go when the breaking news rolls your way. You'll make air on both stories, and can be proud of them, too. Oh, and you'll impress the folks you need to along the way. As an added bonus, you'll have the time to get your facts straight so you don't face any lawsuits. Another day down, and you're continuing your way on up to a larger market and a bigger paycheck.

Our "Into Practice" chapter, which begins on page 135, will give you some great ways to stretch your deadline muscles.

Time is not on your side. Make the most of every tick of the clock.

12

WRITING TIPS

Video and sound are just a few of the ingredients of a television story. Major ingredients, mind you, but not the entire recipe. To make any story complete you need to add a voice track with information that ties the video and sound together. That's where writing comes in. Good writing can make a story sing. Bad writing can, well, make everything fall flat. So, remember what you're about to read. And, use it every time with every story.

> "If you don't like to write, or you don't think it's important and aren't willing to try new ways to improve it, this isn't the profession for you."
> Erin Crowley, producer, KDVR Fox31 News, Denver

WHY THIS STORY?

Start by asking yourself this question. What makes this story so important that the station is dedicating precious airtime to broadcast it? You need to figure this one out, because if you don't care, it will be awfully difficult to make anyone else care.

Once you've answered that one, try this one: *WIIFM*. What's in it for me? The people watching the newscast want to know the answer. How does what you're showing them affect them? Few stories in any newscast affect the general population. Most local news fare consists of stories on shootings, wrecks, fires, and the like—stories that affect a specific group of people in a specific area of town. That's why WIIFM is important. Find the aspect of your story with the broadest appeal and go with it. For instance, many people may not care too much about a story about people dumping their garbage on the roadside. But if you let them know how much it costs them as a taxpayer to clean it up, you've found a broader hot button. When a local apartment complex catches on fire, look for an emotional, human element to help you tell the story. Find some neighbors who have lost their home or focus on the rescue effort. Maybe a firefighter saved a life? Or, the old car wreck story. Is there a way this kind of accident can be avoided in the future? Or, say there's a hydroplaning car during a rainstorm. How can your viewers benefit from this story? Let them know the dangers of driving in the rain, how to keep their own family safe. Those are the kinds of things that make a story memorable. Make it your mission to find and use them every day.

In the same token, if you're profiling a single person or family to personalize a point, keep it in perspective. Often, we take the most extreme cases, and profile them. That's okay, as long as you point out in your story that not every case turns out this way.

THE BASICS

Beginning, Middle, End

How many times have you heard this one? And many stories still don't contain each part. A lot of reporters start their story with the package, then add the anchor lead-in and tag as an afterthought. People aren't going to watch only the package, they'll see the lead-in first (beginning), then the package (middle), and finally the anchor tag (end), as an entire story. Get into this habit. Otherwise, your stories will be disjointed and will most likely repeat themselves. The reporter will end up putting all the information into the package, then can't think of anything else to say. Don't underestimate the importance of the lead-in. If it falls flat, viewers will turn away. So your award-winning package wasn't watched by anyone, because no one cared enough about the lead-in to stay tuned.

> Read all, and we mean *all,* your copy out loud. Your writing is meant to be heard, and the only ones reading it are the anchors.

Write Like You Talk

So easy to say, so hard to do. We mentioned this earlier and think we should mention it again. Television is more personal than newspapers. That's why it's important to make stories more like a conversation. Pretend you're telling your story to your best friend, one on one.

Instead of:

"According to investigators, three bank robbers evaded authorities following a high-speed chase down interstate 40."

(Would you say that to a friend? Probably not.)

Try:

"Police say three bank robbers slipped through their fingers when patrol cars lost them in a high-speed chase down interstate 40."

Instead of:

"Officials say summer barbecues may be the cause of the forest fire."

Try:

"Firefighters say hot coals from summer barbecues may be what sparked the wildfire."

Read It Out Loud

A newsroom at any given time should have reporters, anchors, and producers all reading stories out loud. You'd be amazed at how many silly things you'll catch when you hear what you've written. Besides, the copy is meant to be heard, not read. This will also help you with our last point, being conversational. If a sentence makes you take a breath to read the entire thing out loud, cut it in two, or maybe three. Also, for beginners working on delivery, reading out loud will help you develop a more relaxed style, more like you're talking to your viewers, not telling them something. Many times, the difference between small market news and large market is not just a stilted delivery: it's writing. If the writing isn't conversational, then the best anchor in the market won't be able to read it without stumbling or sounding like he or she is reading.

One Thought, One Sentence

This point will help you with being conversational. Don't overload the viewer with tons of information in a long, run-on sentence that may contain everything you think they need to know but may be too long for them to comprehend and come away with any understanding of what the story was about. See what we mean? Keep it simple and to the point. It's called *tight* in TV news. And, if you master a tight script you're well on your way to becoming a newsroom asset.

If you have too much information in a sentence, viewers will tune out, the worst thing that can happen to you. And if viewers tune out, all that work you did all day long is wasted. Don't confuse them. Keeping it tight will help to make you a more effective communicator.

Filter Your Information

To keep scripts tight, you'll need to determine which information is really necessary to the story. If you're doing a story about a car accident, information about the make, model, year, and color of the cars is extraneous. So is the license plate, *unless* it's a hit-and-run situation, and the police are looking for a certain type of vehicle. You'll need to decide what is pertinent for each story. But a good rule of thumb is, don't let too many facts get in the way of telling the viewer what happened.

Write to Video

This is a must. *View the video before you write the story.* An old-time maxim calls it "See dog, say dog." It sounds logical, doesn't it? Well, many television reporters, writers, and producers don't do it. There's nothing worse than talking about one thing and seeing another on the screen. You'll confuse your viewers. And again, they'll tune out . . . your efforts will be wasted. Sometimes it's difficult to remember that viewers don't know as much as we do about the story. A common mistake is to assume the viewers are thinking what you are. Make sure you aren't jumping to conclusions, showing one thing, but writing three steps ahead.

And, make sure the video matches the *tone* of your story. A beginning reporter made an amateur mistake in her first job that she never forgot. She'd covered the county commission meeting in the morning. Later on that day, a county jail inmate was found attempting to hang himself on the jail exercise equipment. He was taken outside, where someone administered CPR. The news crew got this on tape, and also a bite from a county commissioner about what happened. Back at the station, facing deadline, the reporter used a portion of the earlier county commission meeting for cover video. That's fine, but the shot she selected was of the commissioners laughing (remember the meeting took place before the suicide.) Over that, the voice track was talking about the suicide of a jail inmate. A call from one of the commissioners set her straight, and a valuable lesson was learned.

Once Is Enough

Remember, as we've said time is precious, so don't waste it by repeating yourself. Have you ever heard this one: when an anchor tosses to a soundbite, ". . . and Bill Jones says he's happy he's home . . . ," only to hear Bill Jones on tape say, ". . . I'm so happy to be home. . . ."? Do yourself and your viewers a favor. Look at every frame of video and listen to every word of sound. Then write your story.

Writing to soundbites isn't easy, especially if the person on tape didn't state a complete thought. That's where artistic writing can really bring a story alive.

Make It Flow

Make sure your soundbite completes a thought. Changing gears going into a piece of tape is disconcerting and stops the story cold. Like this:

Anchor: "Witnesses say they ran for cover when the car veered into the crowd."

State patrol officer soundbite: "The driver is identified as 24-year-old Alva Adams. She's in critical condition at St. Mary's Hospital at this time."

See how that got off the thought? Don't pick a bite like that, anyway. You can tell the facts, your bites can tell the emotion, the story. Try this:

Anchor: "People in the crowd ran for cover when the car veered into the crowd."

Witness soundbite: "I grabbed my daughter and got out of the way. I saw that big oak tree and got behind it just in time . . . it happened so fast."

Anchor: "Police say the driver of the car is 24-year-old Alva Adams of Bloomsburg. She's in critical condition."

Make It Active

The whole idea behind television news is immediacy. We can go live and newspapers can't. Passive writing kills that immediacy. So, write actively . . . in the moment.

Instead of:

Protestors have been throwing rocks and bottles at the SWAT team.

Try:

Protestors pelted SWAT officers with rocks and bottles.

Instead of:

Twenty-five-year-old Joe Smith was arrested.

Try:

Police arrested twenty-five-year-old Joe Smith.

Go back to your junior high grammar class. Subject-verb-object. Person A (subject) did (verb) something (object of verb). It's an easy formula.

Another easy formula: active sentences require active verbs. Active verbs say or do something. Passive ones use words like "was arrested," "have been doing," and so on.

By putting the action in the hands of someone in your story you give it life. The words meld with the video. They move. And, they make the story strong and memorable.

Another grammatical mistake we see all the time is the misunderstanding of the difference between *less* and *fewer*. Fewer refers to numbers. If you can count an object, use fewer. Fewer people, fewer cars, fewer concert tickets. . . .

But, if you can't count the object, use less. Less water, less space. There are a few exceptions, like the expression "less than zero," but this is the general rule of thumb.

FIVE THINGS TO AVOID AT ALL COSTS

Like clichés. Here's our favorite no-no list:

1) Up in smoke
2) Scene of the crime
3) In the nick of time
4) Long, hot summer
5) You'd be surprised
6) Adding insult to injury
7) What the future holds.

So many clichés, so little time. Oops!

Avoid slang. No *dissin'* instead of *disrespecting*. No *hangin' ten* instead of *surfing*. And, no *bustin' a move* instead of *dancing*. This is not to say that all slang is unacceptable. For instance, in some television markets it's okay to say *cops* instead of *police*. Or it may be okay to say *bucks* instead of *dollars*. Just use your best judgment and when in doubt, ask someone else for his or her opinion.

And, leave the newspaper news writing to the newspaper reporters. Shy away from using phrases and words like:

1) According to
2) So-and-so said
3) Suffered an injury
4) Flee or fled
5) Blaze

There are many more. Start your own list and refer to it, often.

Finally, avoid news-speak. How often, when you're talking to your significant other or to friends do you use these words?

Residents
Vehicles
Youths
Male/female
Area
Armed

Probably not very often. So don't do it in your scripts. Instead of *residents,* use *neighbors,* or *people who live there.* Instead of *vehicle,* say *car, truck, SUV.* Instead of *youths,* you can substitute *students, a crowd of people, teenagers,* and so on. Instead of *male/female,* it's obvious: *man* or *woman.*

And maybe most important, don't use the terrible trio: *allegedly, apparently, suspects.* These three are perhaps the most overused and least correctly used words in television news. Here's why:

Allegedly: An anchor reads the following over video of a car wreck. "Bumper-to-bumper back-up on Interstate 35 following a three-car pile-up. That's after the driver of a semi-truck allegedly cut across five lanes of traffic." The anchor just told everybody watching that the semi-truck caused the wreck. Wow! Think of the savings! No need for police or insurance companies to investigate any further, the "facts" have already been broadcast.

Wrong! It's better to *attribute* the details of the wreck to somebody. Where did you get the information from? Witnesses? A police officer on the scene, over the phone, or via a faxed statement? Then say that. "Bumper-to-bumper back-up on Interstate 35 following a three-car pile-up. . . . Police say it all started when a semi-truck cut across five lanes of traffic."

You won't be so tempted to use the word *allegedly,* if you look it up in the dictionary. It means to "assert without proof." You can't do that on air. Not unless you're quoting claims from a legal document filed in a lawsuit or other court action. Aside from that, attribute *everything* in *every* story. Otherwise, you may find yourself and your station headed to court. (See chapter 10 for more on the legality of *allegedly.*)

Apparently: Strike this one from your vocabulary list, too. Apparently, *apparently* is just as bad as *allegedly.* A reporter is live outside city hall where the mayor has just announced a crackdown on drivers who double park. "Drivers who double park could apparently face up to a 150-dollar fine." They'll either face the fine or they won't. Find out. Then tell your viewers. "The parking police say drivers who double park face up to a 150-dollar fine."

Suspects: Have you ever heard this one? "The unknown suspect is believed to be somewhere in the tri-county area." There is no such thing as an "unknown suspect." A suspect is a known person who is wanted for, charged with, in jail for, or under investigation in connection with a crime. For someone to be a suspect, they must be known to the police. If detectives have security videotape from a convenience store robbery where a man with a gun is holding up the cashier, then you can say *suspect.* If police release a composite drawing, a face that you can broadcast, then you can say *suspect.* If witnesses positively identified the man who carjacked them as their cousin Bill, and police confirm they are looking for him, then you can say *suspect.* Until then, try easy and accurate script fixes like these:

Instead of:

"Police say a suspect fired shots . . ."

Try:

"Police say the gunman fired shots . . ."

Instead of:

"The suspect got away with the money . . ."

Try:

"The thief ran out with the cash . . ."

TELL AND SHOW

We told you to write to video. You're probably asking, "what if there is limited video?" Good question. Many stories just aren't visual, which is unfortunate, because that's what TV is all about. Nowadays, stations have graphics packages that are good, and graphic artists. If you have limited video for a crime story, say just a shot of the house where it occurred, and a mug shot, why not use a graphic? Maybe list a timeline of what happened. Like this:

8 P.M. Witnesses hear woman screaming.
8:30 P.M. Neighbors see red Jeep driving away.
11 P.M. Suspect is seen at fast food restaurant.
1 A.M. Husband returns home, finds body.

Or anytime you have a list of things, do a graphic—like a list of charges brought against a suspect, or a list of new water restrictions within city limits.

For financial information, it's good to have a graphic to reinforce what the anchor is saying, rather than prolonging a shot of the state legislature. Maybe something like this:

Approved $15 billion budget
$1.5 billion for light rail
$7.5 billion for two new jails, crime prevention program

PUT IT INTO PERSPECTIVE

Numbers and statistics are tricky. Nothing turns viewers glassy-eyed faster than hearing a jumble of numbers or statistics that don't mean anything. Sometimes, taking that extra few minutes to make a phone call to the right person can bring it all together for viewers, and make them say "oh yeah," or "oh wow," instead of dozing off.

What if you're doing a story on water restrictions? The city council passes an emergency ordinance that will charge homes for using more than 10,000 gallons a month. Well, how much is that? Call a local rec center or pool cleaning service. Ask them how much 10,000 gallons is. If they say it's the equivalent of five swimming pools, there you have it. It's a lot easier to visualize five swimming pools than 10,000 gallons of water. If your station has a great graphics department, maybe the graphic artists can make a graphic of five swimming pools. If not, check with the desk to see if a photographer can go and shoot some video of the local swimming pool. You don't need to go; this is something the photog can handle while you're writing the story.

Or how about a story of someone with heart disease walking around neighborhoods, talking to people about this issue. If he walks twenty-five miles a day, and he's been doing it every day for two years, how far is that? Use your computer calculator. 18,250 miles. That's three-fourths of the way around the Earth. Much more effective.

THE TRUTH ABOUT STATISTICS

Statistics are a great device, but it's important to keep in mind that they can be very misleading. Saying that mountain lion attacks in your town have doubled may be alarming. But when you find out there was just one last year and two this year, keep it in perspective. Your viewers should probably be concerned about the hiking trails, but they shouldn't be frightened away.

Get a handle on crime statistics. Every once in a while, the police will release a report on crime trends. "Overall crime up 25 percent in the past five years," could be a typical police press release. Is it true? Actually talk to someone in the department before you parrot back the information to concerned viewers. It could be that *violent* crime is actually holding steady, but other types of crimes, like car theft, have increased. Check it out. A lot of people or organizations use the press release to give out only the information they want to. Dig to find more.

LESS IS MORE

The best writers don't have much to say. Really. Keeping it short and simple not only saves time, it may save viewers as well. Keep the literary stuff for novelists. Here's a great line that's memorable, and very simple. "War ages presidents." What else do you have to say about the ravages of war and the ravages of being at the helm during war? Nothing. It's all there in three little words. Watch some really great writers, like those on CBS *Sunday Morning,* or NBC's Bob Dotson. They are fantastic, and the genius of it all is that they get the point across without laboring the point. Get it. Try it. Nothing will add power to your writing like short, strong sentences.

WRITING TEASES

This isn't as easy as it seems. How hard can it be to summarize an entire story in five to eight seconds, without giving away the best part, just telling enough to entice viewers to watch the story minutes from now . . . and make it catchy and captivating while making sure it matches the video? As we said, it's not easy.

Good tease writing, in fact, is an art. A good tease can make all the difference in whether your audience stays or goes.

Here's an example of two teases written for the same story. There's been a drought all season, and the story is about draining a popular reservoir to keep up with water usage.

> "They're draining the Queenstown Reservoir. We'll tell you why, next."

and

> "A favorite watering hole may be off limits for the rest of the summer. We'll tell you where the fish won't be biting, when we come back."

Which one will keep you watching? Probably the second one. The first one has already told us the entire story, really. Queenstown Reservoir is closing. But the second one will keep you hanging around to see *which* reservoir will be closed. As a bonus, it throws in the crux of the issue . . . you as a viewer will be affected by not being able to swim or fish at a popular summer hangout. You'll stick around to see what the story is about; you are "teased." See what we mean?

However, some information is required to keep the viewers interested. It's not enough to say:

"The president makes a speech tonight, the details at 11."

Boring! Presidential speeches tend to be that way. Remember the WIIFM? Use it now.

"The president's speech tonight may mean some changes for your wallet. That's tonight at 11."

Hmm . . . a little more detail, that affects me, says the viewer. What kind of changes, are taxes going up, is there going to be a tax refund? Better watch and find out. Much more effective.

Always remember the reason for the tease . . . to tease the viewers and keep them tuned in, never more important now, in an age of five hundred channels at the touch of a remote.

AND FINALLY

Look around, observe people, places, and things. A good observer, a good listener, will be a good writer.

YOUR TURN

Watch two stories on the same topic on different channels and see how the respective reporters handle them. Here's an example: the rush to the post office to mail cards and packages just before Christmas. Every year the post office will send your assignment desk the press release stating that "today is the busiest day of the year for the post office. A record 63 million pieces of mail will be sent this year. That includes 23.5 million holiday packages. And an estimated 14 thousand people will pass through the downtown mail facility between 7 A.M. and 10 P.M. today, the extended hours for the holiday season." The assignment desk sends a crew, and sets up a live shot at one of the facilities that's open during the late news, so there's some activity behind the reporter. How would you write this story?

We already mentioned how to handle the facts and figures, but is there another angle to this story that may have more of a WIIFM value?

Here's what we saw; two different stories, the same pieces of information, yet one was much more effective than the other. Two words: forethought and WIIFM. One station found a reporter doing the same old thing . . . repeating back to the viewers the statistics listed in the press release. XXX million packages sent, XXX million pieces of mail through the machines, XXXX people in line at just this one facility alone. Before the end of the story, viewers can't even remember what the reporter said. She could have saved herself the work and just said, "A lot of people mailing a lot of things here today." That's basically all you as the viewer will get from this story.

The second report, on the other hand, was quite different. This reporter put some thought into what he was doing. His live stand-up showed people behind him, but he also showed something more: a tattered piece of mail. The story dealt with the XXX million pieces of mail, but it also showed how putting anything in an envelope can stop the entire process. A bite from a postal worker showed all the things that stopped the machine that day, a candy cane, some change someone sent to a small child, a folded piece of notebook paper inside a card from a student to relatives back home. None of those cards or letters made it to their destinations. The machines ate them. People at Christmas time are tempted to slip little surprises in envelopes, then are surprised when the mail never makes it. The envelopes get eaten by the high-speed, super thin mail chutes that allow XXXX million pieces a day.

So here's a story that contained all the facts, plus much more . . . how to make sure your mail actually makes it to its destination, that is to say, news you can use.

All it takes is a little imagination, and a few minutes of contemplation. How will this story affect my viewers? How can I make them care, especially if they were the majority of people who *didn't* go the post office today? This reporter really hit the nail on the head.

> Think of your story as a drop in a pond. It has a ripple effect. Will it sink in without notice? Or will it ripple outward, affect others, and be meaningful to your viewing audience?

13

INTO PRACTICE

Now, here's your chance to put yourself in the shoes of journalists who face dilemmas day in and day out. We've come up with some scenarios that could happen at any time. Think about what you'd do, and get prepared to hit the ground running. For the first example we used a real-life experience; we describe what actually happened and how the challenges were met. Then you're on your own, as we give some examples of what could happen.

THE CHASE

A man had just led police on a high-speed chase through two cities, reaching speeds of one hundred miles per hour. Along the way, he tried to run officers off the road, they fired on him, he caused three wrecks, tried to ditch the car he was driving and carjack two others, and finally, slammed head-on into a power pole. In the end, he ran to a nearby convenience store, where police arrested him without incident. All this happened one hour before news time. The reporter had precious little time to make sure he had video, sound, and accurate information.

Two problems: short staffing at the station left the photographer and the reporter alone, and police media representatives were unusually short on information. They were faced with the daunting task of shooting a story, writing and editing it, setting up a live shot, feeding back the story to the station, and getting ready for a live story hit at the top of the show, as this was breaking news.

What to do? The clock is ticking. The reporter took a quick inventory of what he had. There was great arrest video, showing the man police had chased through the streets of the city, bloodied by gunfire, on his knees, as officers handcuffed him and paramedics prepared him for a trip to the hospital. Video, got it. Then there were the dozens of witnesses watching it all happen. The crew quickly spotted a couple who, for better or worse, had joined in the chase early on and had followed it through until the end. Interview 1, got it. And finally, the police PIO showed up. Interview 2, got it.

The reporter ran back to the live truck, and logged and wrote the story, while the photographer set up the live shot. The story was edited and fed back to the station; and the crew barely made its slot. This is an extreme example of being on your own, but it happens, and you must be prepared for it. The truth is, it's just one in a seemingly endless stream of situations you must be able to navigate in order to craft a story and make it on the air.

Now it's your turn. Imagine yourself in the following situations. Discuss how you would handle them on the job as a reporter, producer, photographer, or assignment editor. Write down your ideas, your plans, and always keep in mind you're working under deadline pressure. Then check out our advice.

SITUATION #1: SHOOTING

It's one hour before show time. The assignment desk hears scanner traffic describing a shooting, what sounds like three people dead, including a child. A crew heads to the scene. The live truck and engineer are gearing up. The producer wants a live shot at the top of the show. When the crew arrives, they find yellow crime scene tape, police milling about gathering evidence and too busy to talk to reporters, and neighbors standing around, some crying.

Formulate a coverage plan on your feet. How would you best gather accurate information, video, and sound, and capture the emotion of what's happening? You have thirty minutes to meet your deadline for air. Go at it.

SITUATION #2: CITY COUNCIL

The city council is likely to pass a new ordinance that will double fines for dog owners who don't clean up after their pets in public parks. On one side, you have people, including an outspoken council member, who say they're pooped out over the poop. They say it's time for pet owners to pick it up or pay. On the other side, you have pet owners who say the city is barking up the wrong tree. They say they are the targets of overzealous city leaders who are looking for a way to run them and their pets out of city parks. The council votes tonight. How do you cover this story? The producer wants a live shot on this controversial issue.

SITUATION #3: THE COURTS

It's your first time covering a high-profile murder trial. You're clued into the particulars of the case, but you hear there are restrictions on media coverage at the courthouse. Set up your coverage plan. Who do you call for information on media access to the courthouse? Can you have cameras in the courtroom? In the hallways? What are the rules and how can you best cover the story and follow them at the same time?

OUR ADVICE

Situation #1: Shooting

Hit the ground running.

Field crew: It's important that the reporter and photographer work together. Discuss what each will do first after arriving on scene. Once the crew arrives at the scene, split up. Find out if the scanner traffic was accurate, and if it's a legitimate story. Relay this information back to the station as soon as possible. The photographer looks for the best shots, the reporter heads for the best and most accurate information and interviews. Find a police officer. Ask investigating officers if there's a PIO on scene. Officers won't give you information on their own. If there's no PIO, ask for the officer in command. Next, find reliable witnesses. Neighbors, passersby . . . but keep in mind, some people just want to be on TV. Use your judgment as to whether these people are reliable. There may even be family members of the victims or shooter on scene. Ask around, and be assertive, but not intrusive.

Once you've taped the video and the interviews, head back to the live truck. The reporter can view tape and write the story accordingly. The photographer can be setting up the live truck, then editing the story, and feeding back tape. With luck, you'll hit your time slot.

Assignment desk: The assignment desk should continue to gather as much accurate information as possible, by talking to police dispatchers, paging the PIO (you can also set up an interview with the PIO and the reporter out in the field to meet), and keeping an ear on the scanner and relaying that information to the reporter. Keep in mind, scanner traffic is oftentimes unreliable. Never report directly from what you hear on a police scanner—*always confirm this information.* As more pertinent information becomes available, pass it on to the producer and the reporter. Remember, the reporter is trying to look at video and write the story, and is now out of the information-gathering loop. It's up to you to pass on any new information, like the victim's names, and so on.

Producers/writers: The producer will be waiting for crew to call back to confirm if this is still a leadable story. Then he or she will change the entire show and the rundown to reflect this change, and notify everyone involved, such as graphics, the director, the anchors, engineers, and management. Producer will need enough information from either the assignment desk or the field crew to write a headline tease and an intro to toss to the reporter. Producer must work with engineering to make sure the live shot will be there technically, and with the field crew to make sure they will be able to make their slot. Producer must ascertain whether the reporter will be sending back a package, a VO, a VO/SOT, or a straight live without tape, and get roll cues for tape. Associate producers/writers will assist in any way with gathering information for the producer.

Situation #2: City Council

Field crew: You may want to start at the source, for example, the park. Find a pet owner and her dog. Some cities and neighborhoods even have dog playgroups where man's best friends get together for fetch and fetching conversation. In any case, find someone you feel confident you can convince to be part of your story. Talk to the pet owner about whether she picks up after her pooch and whether it bothers her when others don't. Then find someone who couldn't care less. Maybe he lets his dog go wherever it wants and never picks up the mess. Or find someone who doesn't understand why this is such a hot-button issue. Talk to the city councilperson sponsoring the new ordinance. Get the specifics from the proposed legislation, especially about how much it will cost people, if they get caught not picking up after their pets. Shoot your video and interview the people in the park . . . this is the best backdrop. Think about your live shot, it could be in the park; maybe you could walk and talk with a dog on a leash. Don't forget to have someone from council notify you immediately about the vote on the pet poop issue, if you don't have the time to attend the meeting.

Assignment desk: Make calls before the reporter gets in. Set up interviews with the city councilperson and with pet owners, if you can find any. Ask the councilperson's assistant to fax you a copy of the proposed ordinance. Check if any council people are against the ordinance, and contact them, too. Basically, any legwork you can do for the reporter will help.

Producers/writers: Producer must decide how important this story is in relation to all the other news of the day. Granted, it's probably the most recent thing happening for the late newscast, but it may not be a lead. Keep in touch with the field crew to get their feeling on the issue. Are the people they are talking to finding this controversial, or do they not really care? What do they have for the live shot tonight? A package, a VO/SOT, a VO? Make sure the reporter or desk person notifies you, as soon as the vote comes down.

Situation #3: The Courts

Field crew: All courts operate differently. The most important thing any reporter can do is find out what the court's rules are regarding electronic media coverage, or EMC. Can you have a camera in the courtroom, in the hallways, in the building, or only on the sidewalk outside? Call the clerk of court or the district attorney's office to find out. Oftentimes, the judge will make the final decision. Your station may have to file special paperwork to cover certain court cases. Find out *before* you go.

Assignment desk: Keep files of court dates for high-profile cases. You must file ahead of time for EMC. Make your own calls to the clerk of court to make sure nothing has changed, like a guilty plea, or that the trial date has once again been moved. Keep a file of all background information on this case. It could come in handy for a reporter who isn't familiar with every aspect of the case.

Producers/writers: Producer must again decide how this story weighs in with others of the day. Keep in touch with the reporter to see what's going on. A B-block lead may become an A-block live shot lead if something dramatic happens, such as compelling testimony, or a sudden guilty plea, or quick verdict. Be ready for anything, and have at least an outline of a Plan B in your mind if something breaks.

Now let's take some time to see what it's like to write a story under deadline pressure. You have five minutes to write this story, print it out, and run it into the studio, to the producer's booth, and to the director. That means you really have about three minutes to write. Here are the facts:

There's been a car accident. A police car is involved. The police PIO says the officer is in critical condition at St. Mary's Hospital. He was going down 13th Avenue southbound, when a black Ford Mustang, 1999 model, was coming down Maple Street. The driver of the car failed to stop at the stop sign and ran into the police cruiser. The driver of the car is nineteen-year-old John Smith, who has a suspended license. There were two other occupants in the car, but they were ejected. One died, and the other was taken to St. Mary's Hospital, in serious condition. They appear to be young men, but their identities haven't been released. The driver is listed in serious condition, also. The accident happened at 9:07 this evening. The officer is identified as Joe Parker, a ten-year veteran of the force. He was going to check out an assault call at 2102 South Street.

You write the story, but the producer says there's only twenty seconds to spare, so you have to keep it to that time. Start now.

> You can't prepare for every situation, because news will always throw you a curve ball. Keep your cool, think fast, and don't say anything you don't want repeated back to you!

14

NEWS QUIZ: TEST YOUR KNOWLEDGE OF HISTORY, RECENT EVENTS, AND PEOPLE

As we've said before, working in TV news is like being a modern Renaissance person. You need to know at least a little, if not more, about a lot of different subjects and issues. You can really get burned if you don't do this. In layman's terms, don't get caught with your pants down.

Here's an example: One green reporter was set to interview the local Middle East expert about an Israeli-Palestinian crisis. She intended to ask about what had happened on the West Bank, but instead she said the Left Bank. The Left Bank is famous for harboring budding artists in Paris. Quite a difference! Needless to say, the interview was over before it had really started, and the reporter's credibility was sorely damaged with a valuable contact that she would need again in the future.

Here's how to avoid that situation. Simple: know your stuff. If you know you'll be doing a story on a certain topic, read up. Even a few minutes on a topic will gain you a little knowledge to ask intelligent questions. But, if you're working on the fly and absolutely don't know what you're talking about, make the person you're interviewing feel like the star. Start the interview by saying that you need a little background information on what's going on. Use your head, though. Don't ask the governor for background information. If you don't know, this is one of those times where you have to think on your feet and wing it. Better yet, just don't get caught in this position with a person of importance. Here's how to keep on your toes for anything that comes your way.

The following quiz isn't a hard-and-fast test for anyone entering television news. But because as an assignment editor, producer, reporter, or anchor, you'll need to know a little about a lot of different subjects, and sound like you know even more, here's a starting point.

1. Name at least one town/city council person, and a county commissioner in your market.
2. Who are the state legislators representing your market?
3. Who are your Congress people and senators?
4. Name at least two members of the president's cabinet and which department they head up.
5. What does "no contest" mean in court?
6. Who were the Little Rock Seven?
7. Who shot Lee Harvey Oswald, and what year did this occur?
8. Which president used the term "voodoo economics," and what does this mean?
9. Name three leaders of Middle East countries.
10. Which countries are part of the G-7? What is the eighth country that is included in the yearly talks?
11. Which countries are included in NATO, and what is this organization all about? Is the United States a member?
12. What's NAFTA, and why is it a hot-button issue periodically?
13. What was the Vietnam conflict all about?
14. What was the Watergate scandal all about?
15. Who are the religious leaders in your community?

Just because you're not a reporter or anchor doesn't mean you don't need to have a well-rounded set of knowledge.

Assignment editors, you're the gatekeeper of information for the newsroom and may well be the first contact someone has with your station. A major stumble over the phone may change an important person's mind about giving you a story. Or you may completely miss a story because you don't think it is one.

Producers, you too could completely miss the story. Misjudging its importance could make you place a very important story way down in the newscast, or maybe drop it altogether. You don't want to end up telling your news director why you didn't think a certain story was important. Or you could misunderstand a story. You write the teases, you make the errors. Take the time a producer wrote a tease for a story on a B-52 bomber on display at a local museum. She didn't ask or take the time to understand what the story was all about. She wrote that the "workhorse of World War II" was on display. Unfortunately, the B-52 wasn't even used in WW II. Imagine how the phone lines lit up in that newsroom! Or the producer who wrote about the gun that fired the shot that killed JFK in Dallas. The tease video showed a tiny handgun. Imagine how the producer felt when everyone made jokes about long-range handguns. The gun was actually the one used by Jack Ruby to shoot Lee Harvey Oswald, JFK's assassin. That five-second tease was the butt of newsroom jokes for a lot longer than five seconds.

Reporters and anchors, your face is on the screen. Enough said. At least assignment editors, producers, and writers can cringe behind the camera. But you can't. What if spot news comes along during the show you're anchoring? Say the Majority Leader of the U.S. Senate dies, whether from a heart attack or is murdered. What's that person's name? How long in office? Other details about him? Do you want to be the parrot who is fed the generic information from the AP wire on the producer's computer, through your ear? Or would you rather know your stuff? Same for reporters. What if that event happened while the senator was speaking in your hometown? You'd go on live, and you'd have even less access to background information out there in the field than an anchor. See how any type of national or international news may suddenly become a big issue in your backyard? And see why it's important to always be prepared? Just a little bit of information can go a long way.

Will you be prepared the next time a huge news story comes your way and you just happen to be in the middle of it? We've listed some websites, books, and periodicals at the end of this book in the

"Going Online" section to help you keep up on issues and to get background information. But sometimes the best way to get the feeling of what happened is just plain old-fashioned. Talk to people . . . be interested in people . . . find out their stories. Respect older people. They were there, and they have firsthand information. People at news stations have hidden talents and backgrounds. Some we know personally have risked their lives in Vietnam, have traveled the world, been part of the military or law enforcement, have parents who escaped Nazi Germany, grew up on farms, are independently wealthy, know the president personally, and have hobbies like playing music, knowing everything there is to know about any plane ever made, any car ever made, any machine ever made, some are storm chasers, and so on. Some are old movie buffs, World War II buffs, history buffs, opera buffs, travel buffs, TV buffs, you name it. There is a goldmine just sitting in your newsroom, and with the people you come in contact with every day. Think of them as being your secret weapon, a hidden treasure. That B-52 producer we mentioned could have talked to the plane buff and not have had the agony of discrediting her station on the air.

So, the information is out there, it's just up to you to mine it, organize it, and buff it into that beautiful gem that was a diamond in the rough.

Here's how to keep yourself polished, like that diamond: Read at least part of two periodicals and newspapers a day. This means above and beyond your local newspapers. The *Wall Street Journal* is a wealth of information, plus daily news. Select something you're interested in, and then expand. There are so many periodicals, hard copy and online, that there really isn't an excuse not to do this. When you get into work, before the assignment meeting, log on. Read, read, read. You will never go wrong. And remember, you can never have too much information. It will serve you well.

15

WORST-CASE SCENARIOS

No matter how hard you work to get that exclusive interview, no matter how perfectly you stack the show, no matter how quickly you funnel new information to the reporter, things will fall apart. It's a fact of life in a television newsroom. The show will implode. It's nobody's fault. Well, sometimes it is. But, most of the time, what seems like angry gods doing everything possible to screw up a newscast is actually one minor mistake that snowballs into a major catastrophe. It's inevitable, it's aggravating, and believe us, it will happen.

When it happens, you have two choices.

1) Fall apart.
2) Learn and move on.

Case in point. This actually happened. It was two hours to news time. The producer had the show stacked, written, pretty much ready to go. The assignment desk was enjoying a rare moment of calm. The reporters and photographers were in-house or out in the field putting the finishing touches on their stories. Then it happened. An air tanker working to put out a forest fire broke apart in midair and went down, killing all aboard. It was scramble time. The producer immediately went to work restacking the show to accommodate the new top story. The assignment desk kicked into overdrive working to gather as much information as possible about the crash and redirecting field crews to the scene (which of course was in a fairly remote area). A reporter, a photographer, and a satellite truck and operator were already covering the fire, so they were on scene. That was a plus, or so it seemed. Turns out the truck operator and photographer left the reporter, alone, with the sat truck just minutes before the plane went down. They left to shoot some extra video and pick up some food in a nearby town. The problem is, when the plane crashed the police immediately shut down the road. At that point, even authorities didn't know exactly what just happened, or what was going on. They too were scrambling. Result: the crew was trapped on the wrong side of the roadblock! That left the reporter by herself with no way to go live from the scene of the crash. No problem, the assignment editor thought. A second crew was headed to the scene from the other side and they'd be able to help her out. Plus, another truck operator was on the way. Problem solved, right? Wrong. The second crew and the new truck operator arrived, but the satellite truck died. It wouldn't work. A mechanical problem. Now what? The show still had to go on. The news team still had to report on the crash somehow. But how, with no video and no live shot? One word: *phoner*. Both reporters at the scene of the crash had to report via telephone. No video, no interviews on tape. Just the reporters, on the phone, reporting on the crash and eyewitness accounts. The graphics department had built a map of the crash location, and made a timeline list of what was known to have led up to the crash. Not the most desirable option, but the only one available at the time. Everything that could go wrong, pretty much did. But, the news team kept it together and did what they could with what they had.

They learned, too. First and foremost, some things are beyond human control. That includes circumstance and technology. The photographer and sat truck operator could not have known that their short trip would leave them stranded. But, you can bet they won't leave a reporter alone, again. Next time, even if the satellite truck breaks down, they'll be there. Back at the station, the assignment editor and the producer now have experience on how to deal with a catastrophe in the making. And, the reporters now know that they can report on a major breaking story without the aid of video and sound. Almost like the old days.

As the old saying goes, though, what goes around, comes around. Bad news karma one day will end up as good news karma another.

The same news team was the only one with continuous live coverage of yet another breaking news story, another forest fire, that broke out close to a large population area. Turns out a news crew was headed back from a story they'd just done live, when they spotted the fire. They pulled off, got into great position, and were broadcasting live reports (this time with exclusive video!) before the other stations knew what was going on.

Here's another worst-case scenario that didn't turn out so well. This is actually the story of a station that just didn't have it together.

It started out so simply. A simple live broadcast from the scene of a massive flood that killed dozens of people twenty years ago. It's the anniversary and just about anyone who was around at the time can remember that flood. In this case, planning was underway for a few weeks. The station didn't have its own satellite truck, which was a problem because the flood occurred in a canyon, where no microwave signal could be picked up or sent out. The news manager had worked out a deal with another station (let's call them Station 2) for the use of its sat truck. This would seem to work in theory, because the station that owned the truck had a newscast an hour later. So, the crew from Station 1 would get all the bites, edit the story in its own microwave truck, walk it over to the sat truck, feed the story, have the reporter do the live at the top of the show, and that would leave plenty of time for the second station to feed its tape and do its live shot. In theory.

In two words the entire scenario fell apart. Cell phone. No one took into account that if a microwave truck can't transmit out of a canyon, neither can a cell phone. The editor from Station 1 couldn't communicate back to the producer. So, no one back at the station could know when tape was being fed. The editor found a phone booth about one-quarter of a mile away, and called the station to tell them to be ready for the uplink, then walked back to the sat truck and fed the tape. Okay, so it's a hike to communicate with the station. We're talking worst-case scenario, however. There was no audio, and the producer at the station could only sit and watch a great package being fed, with no sound. This is going to sound ludicrous, but the editor had to keep going back and forth, down a dark canyon road, to make calls from a phone booth to try and correct the problem. Needless to say, this took a lot of precious time and didn't work. The producer had to scramble to even get some VO from that day, edit it along with some file of the flood, then write the lead story. The station had a VO, when the others had an entire A-block of coverage.

It might cross your mind to ask how the other stations in the market were able to communicate. Simple: satellite phone. Station 1 wasn't equipped. Stations 2, 3, and 4 in the market were. Why didn't station 2 lend the use of their phone, too? Because they were busy on the phone with their own producers, talking about the coverage they had. And, let's face it, the deal was worked out among management at both stations, not the folks who work in the field. The crew at Station 2 most likely wasn't happy about having to give up their facilities an hour before news time and acted accordingly.

What could Station 1 have done ahead of time to avoid this situation? Two things. They could have thought about the cell phone/sat phone situation, obviously; or rented their own sat truck, which comes equipped with the phone. The money spent would probably have more than paid for the loss of credibility and coverage on a big story. And, finally, Station 1 should not have put everything into the hands of another station, because when it comes down to crunch time, you can't rely on a competitor to help you out. The decisions made by the managers at Station 1 really compromised the entire show. If more thought had been put in ahead of time, this scenario would never have happened. And in this case, a phoner wasn't even an option. All the producer could do at that point was to punt.

Take some time now to think about what you would do if any commonplace things happen, like the computers crashing. You've got a great newscast or a great package, all entered into the computer, but you don't have access. What now?

There's not much to do in this situation but wing it. Most stations now have back-up generators, if electricity is a problem. A good producer will always make everyone in the newsroom save their work and print it out during a thunderstorm. A power hit at the wrong time can be devastating.

Here's another one where a news director overreacted, but his staff kept the ship afloat.

My worst-case scenario is a good one. The verdict was coming down in a huge murder trial and all the stations and the networks were there and we were all going live. We were crammed into a pretty tight space, everything was taped down, there was nowhere to move; if someone leaned into your shot you were stuck. Well, my news director didn't like my camera position, and he went in the control room and got on the headset to me and told me that if I didn't move my shot I would be fired . . . I told him I couldn't move and he fired me while my shot was on the air live. I was in such shock I ignored him and kept shooting and they kept airing it, it wasn't that bad of a shot, and afterward I started crying and told the field producer what had happened, and later that night the assistant news director called me at home to make sure I knew I wasn't really fired. But that news director never mentioned it to me or apologized himself. (Carol Lynde, photographer)

These are just a few examples of worst-case scenarios. There are countless more. And, as long as you work in television news, you too will have the heart-pounding pleasure of experiencing them firsthand. Get ready.

16

AMATEUR ERRORS

Everybody's got to start somewhere. But you don't have to *look* like you are just beginning your first job. Let that be your secret. Here are some things to avoid, for starters, that will make you look greener than the grass patch outside the station.

> "It is not about the mistake, but more about how you recover from it. I lost way too much sleep for missing my first slot as a reporter or for stumbling during a newscast as an anchor. You are a work in progress when you're 'green' at broadcasting."
> Debbie Denmon, anchor

FOR ANYONE WHO WRITES STORIES

The following tips are directed to anyone in the newsroom who writes stories, including reporters, editors, producers, and others.

No Repeat

This is a biggie. Write to the bites in VO/SOTS or packages, but don't repeat what they contain. How many times have you heard this one?

> VO: "The tornado was the largest in the area in years. Witnesses say they've never seen anything like it."

SOT witness: "I've never seen anything like it . . . we ran down to the basement. . . ."

Or this situation from a live shot where an anchor is tossing to a reporter, who will toss to a package:

Anchor: "The city council voted 3 to 2 tonight to pass the ordinance. Channel 5's John Smith is standing by live with more."

John Smith: "That's right Tom, the city council voted 3 to 2 to pass the fireworks ban because of the drought."

Package: "The city council went ahead tonight, voting 3 to 2 to go ahead with the fireworks ban. . . ."

Ugh!! Remember, when you repeat yourself, you are wasting valuable time that you could be using to relay other information. Every moment is valuable.

Watch Your Phrasing

In a story about some kids killed near an old oak tree, for example, don't say, "The victims were shot by the tree." We didn't know that trees were killers.

If Only

Be careful with the word *only* when it comes to victims. This isn't just an amateur error, we hear it all the time. When you say, "five people were killed this year in parachute jumping accidents, as compared to only one last year," how does that sound? If you were the wife or husband of that "only" victim, *only* would seem to trivialize that person's life, and death.

Irony and Coincidence

This is one we see all the time. There's a difference between a coincidence and irony. Coincidence is just that, two separate incidents that coincide. Irony is something that happens that is unexpected or incongruous.

Two family members dying in separate car accidents a week apart isn't ironic, it's a coincidence. Tragic as this is, it's nothing more. You need that sense of incongruity for irony, like James Dean dying in a car accident, due to recklessness, right after he had shot a short film on driving safely. Or a bank robber who gets held up while he's a customer in a bank. Usually, what many people at first consider to be irony is coincidence.

Know Your Stuff

Nothing says "young" and "inexperienced" like a reporter/producer who doesn't know about history or political events in the past. We've addressed this before, but we can say it again. If you want to keep your credibility and avoid becoming that newsroom legend, brush up.

PRODUCERS/WRITERS

These tips are addressed especially to producers and writers.

Writing Teases

Make sure they match the video. Take the tease about the twenty-fifth anniversary of Elvis Presley's death. It said something like, "Twenty-five years after the king dies, Graceland is still rocking the jailhouse." A catchy, short tease, but the video was of some guy walking down the street. Huh? If the video doesn't match, the snappiest tease will fall flat and leave the viewer confused. If that is the only video you have, consider pulling file tape of Elvis or going with a reader tease.

Plan for Change

Always have a backup plan, because things will change. Don't produce yourself into a corner with nowhere to go.

Communicate, communicate, communicate. One of the biggest mistakes inexperienced producers make is assuming everyone else knows what you are doing and thinking. Tell them your plan, then tell them again. Example: tell your reporter that he is scheduled for a live tease, so he won't have the deer-in-the-headlights look when the anchor tosses to him.

Cutline Chaos

If your station requires cutlines with teases (a word or phrase that accompanies the video), make sure the words and the pictures complement each other and make sense. One producer didn't take the time to look at video a photographer had shot of people buying lottery tickets. It isn't the editor's job to look at the graphics list to ensure the words and pictures match up. The cutline on the bottom of the screen was "Big Bucks." The shot the editor selected was the back end of a convenience store clerk handing a customer a lottery ticket. The clerk happened to be very large. Needless to say, the words "Big Bucks" situated right underneath her rear end may have given news staff quite a chuckle when the tease aired, but there could have been a better combination of words and video.

No News-Speak

This is a no-no for cutlines, squeezebacks, and graphics. We mean, don't use words like *Fatal Ax* for an over-the-shoulder cutline. To a viewer who isn't familiar with news jargon (and there are a lot of them out there!), that means an ax murder story, not a car accident. We see this more times than I can believe. *Folo* is another that crops up (instead of follow-up). Or, since news script uses hyphens between letters, like U-S, for easier reading, these tend to come up in the news headlines squeezed back at the bottom of the screen. Example: "U-S weapons inspectors say. . . ." Don't do it! It's an easy habit to get into, but folks at home won't appreciate it.

TALENT

Anchors and on-air personalities, these tips are for you.

To the Point

Avoid long stand-ups. Make these short and sweet—twenty seconds max. Avoid stick mics; they are old-fashioned and don't make you look natural on air. They may be better during windy situations, though, to cut down on the sound of the wind.

Same thing for SOTs. Don't let folks run on. Your audience will fall asleep. Thirty-second SOTs are unacceptable unless you have the most powerful of speakers or emotional of bites. Use SOTs for information that you can't impart on your own. Don't use the cop saying, "The incident occurred at approximately 3 A.M., and the suspect is identified as John Jones, 32 years old, who resides at 15 Maple Street, Apartment 27B." Boring! You can say that stuff yourself. Use the cop saying something like, "Yes, this is an extremely rare case, we don't see this type of crime here in Queensbury all that often." Much better.

When you use someone's name in a story, a suspect, perhaps, put the age first. "Police are looking for 49-year-old Wilma Wilkins." Or, if you use a title (usually for stories that don't have a SOT with that person), put that first, so people won't get confused, thinking, who is Joe Jones? Example: "Joe Jones, the sheriff's detective, says. . . ." Viewers will be thinking about the name and will likely miss why they are mentioned in the story. But if you say, "Sheriff's detective Joe Jones says the suspect is in custody," people will have a frame of reference.

Good Endings

Don't end on a soundbite, then put on your reporter tag. This is just plain lazy. And just because you see this happening in major markets doesn't make this acceptable. End on a soundbite *only* if you can't top it, say, a really emotional bite from a victim, and the like. Or put some nat sound on at the end: "we may never see another flood like it," with nats of rushing water. Then put on your tag, John Smith, News 5.

Keep It to Yourself

We've all heard this one before. Don't say anything with your mic on that you wouldn't want to go over the air. Period. People can lose credibility and jobs over something said when they thought their mics were off. We can't tell you many of these examples, as they are un-printable!

"I had just finished a live shot that was technically a night-mare. I looked at the camera and said, 'What the *&#@* hap-pened?' Needless to say, I was still on the air, the mic was still open, and my expletive was broadcast to an entire audience at noon. My mishap made the *Miami Herald,* front page, local section. I received letters asking me to apologize to the audi-ence. Luckily for me, the PR department for the station did that. I was so fortunate; only got a slap on the hand and sent home. From then on, my mouth stays shut."

Juan Fernandez, reporter

Street Smarts

Don't parrot back what neighbors say. Make sure you check facts. Sometimes neighbors you interview may not know what's going on. If you feel like you really want to use the information, *attribute* it.

Grammar

Don't use singular verbs with plural subjects. Such as, "There's fifty people protesting out here right now." *Fifty* is plural, *there's* or *there is* is singular.

For graphics purposes: know the difference between effect and affect: affect is (mostly) a verb; effect is (mostly) a noun. Hence, I'm affected by the effects of the storm. Look them up. Same thing, get into the habit so you sound educated on your live shots.

Proper Nouns, Please

Whether you're live or not, make sure you address distinguished people properly. A reporter on a live shot once called a powerful senator she was interviewing by the woman's first name. Always say, "Senator, where do you stand on this issue." If you're unsure, use Mr., Mrs., or Ms.

ASSIGNMENT EDITORS:
BE DETAIL-ORIENTED

Follow up on anything, anything that looks like it could be a story. Press releases, phone calls, and so on. Read the entire press release. Don't be the assignment editor who doesn't read the details of the press release, then gets burned.

Get directions to shoots . . . you don't want crews wasting time, driving all over, to find a story. Make the call, get the facts.

PHOTOGRAPHERS AND EDITORS:
POINT OF VIEW

Photographers, or anyone who ends up shooting video, vary your shots. Don't have an entire story full of medium shots, shot from shoulder height. Take the camera off the tripod or raise or lower the tripod if you need to. Get low angles, higher angles. And vary your shots with not just medium shots, but close-ups, extreme close-ups, long shots. Put the camera on the sidewalk and shoot the length of the entire street. Don't be afraid to get close to the people you're talking to. Of course, use good judgment and don't get into someone's face, especially if they're uncomfortable. Sometimes, people will get so wrapped up in their story that they'll forget they're on camera. This is the time to get real close, when the emotion is flowing.

And, don't shoot something you're not supposed to, even if it's all a joke to you. Who knows, it may end up on air.

Take this case. A photographer and a reporter were in court all day. As trials go, this one wasn't bad, but almost all testimony gets extremely boring at some point. The photographer decided to relieve his boredom by taking shots of women's legs in the newsroom. (Nothing profane or obscene, here, just plain shots of professional women in nylons as they were sitting, listening to the testimony.)

It turns out that this boring testimony was leading up to something spectacular at the end of the day. The reporter and photographer rushed back to the station, and the reporter ended up editing the VO portion, because the photographer was called away to shoot something else at the last minute. The reporter had just a few minutes to edit a :30 VO. She knew the photographer was pretty good at editing in the camera, that is, the reporter figured she could just let the raw footage roll, and it would be usable on air. Imagine her surprise and frustration when at :20 in, the shots of women's legs popped up. They almost ended up on air. The anchor would have been saying something about a key witness testifying how she had seen a gang of kids beating up her friend, when shots of the court reporter's and the prosecutor's legs would have been the cover video. What had seemed funny earlier that morning wasn't later on that afternoon.

> Keep calm under pressure, listen and observe others, and be professional at all times. Then acknowledge and learn from your mistakes.

17

GETTING THE JOB

Now that you know what to do on that coveted first job in TV news, how do you go about *getting* that first job?

It's a fine line between persistence and peskiness. Send resumés (and tapes for talent) to markets that you'd like to work in. Make a checklist and call the news director or appropriate person every week. Say you're just checking in. These follow-up phone calls may last just thirty seconds, but your name, resumé, and tape will stay in their heads. Ask anyone how they got their first job. Most will say persistence, some will say luck, and a few will say they just fell into it. A news director can't help but love persistence. If you're that tenacious in just trying to get the job, you'll probably be that way chasing down a story.

Take the case of a wanna-be reporter who made her calls every week. She made her calls one day, after weeks and weeks of calling the same news directors in the same markets. The day after a round of calls, a news director called her back. He'd had two reporters quit that same day. He remembered talking to this job seeker for weeks, and he pulled her tape out of the stack because he talked to her week in and week out. She got the job. The news director knew that this person would likely chase down a story as tenaciously as she chased down the job.

Don't make the excuse not to call. It's easier than ever to find out if jobs are available, who the news director is, and the proper spelling of his or her name. Almost every station in the country has a website with this information. Use it. You and the station will benefit in the end. And *never misspell* a news director's name. If you don't care enough to double-check this, don't bother sending it out. It'll end up in the round file.

When a news director calls you back, be honest and straightforward. It can be intimidating. If you absolutely don't know how to do something, don't lie. If you end up getting hired, everyone will find out soon enough that you don't know what you are doing. And that may do your career much more harm than good. Face it, you can either edit, or you can't. You can write, or you can't. You can handle an assignment desk or you can't. Look at the job descriptions. Is the job for you? If you really want this job and don't have the skills listed, is there a place where you can acquire them? These are the things you'll need to find out.

When you get called in for an interview, dress professionally. Most newsrooms are casual, especially for non-talent. But take it upon yourself to look like a professional. Look at how others are dressed once you are hired. That's the time to look more casual, if that's the norm there, not during the interview. Take a tape and resumé with you (and for associate producers and news writers, some writing samples), even though the news director most likely has the materials you sent. Sometimes, they can't locate them, or they were lent to someone else to look at. Or they're stuck in a pile a mile high and the news director can't find them. You'll practically be expected to bring these things with you. You may have to go over your tape step by step with the news director, and answer questions as to why you did certain things the way you did. Be prepared with answers.

There are as many questions asked as there are news directors. Of course, you'll most likely be asked about your previous experience, whether it's an internship, an entry-level job in a radio or TV station, or a job in a newspaper office. Even working as a receptionist, with no hands-on experience in the newsroom, is still a plus. Turn it around to your advantage. So what if you have to answer the phones, take messages, and properly code employee expense reports? You see the news director every day, plus everyone in the newsroom. Even if there isn't a job there for you, you may find out through those people about other jobs. They all came from smaller stations and have contacts there; their friends have contacts, too, and may know about openings, and what pleases a particular news director they've worked with before. Then, bug the news people to let you observe or help out after your work hours. You've heard of networking . . . now do it. That way, even if you don't actually work in the newsroom, you can impress a potential news director that you really *do* have experience. And that you'll make the most of the opportunities that come your way.

When you walk into a station for an interview, be yourself. Be confident. Crank up your energy a notch, maybe, to make an impression.

A great way to be prepared is to go online. We've listed a lot of websites that show job openings. Some of those even list tips on getting a job, and the cost of living for different markets, so you can compare salary information with how much you'll need to get by.

Have a working knowledge of the market. The news director may throw something out about the city or state you are in, and you'll again need to be prepared. Some stations even give pop quizzes to candidates. Read a newspaper or watch a local newscast before your interview. The mayor's name will most likely be included. A city-sponsored website will, too. Watching the local newscast of the station you're interviewing with will give you a feel as to what's expected of the people who work there. What kind of news do they cover? How do they cover it? Make notes; take them along. It wouldn't hurt to make a suggestion or two as to story ideas. But take care not to be critical of what you've seen on their air. That would probably not go over very well!

And, be prepared for anything. Some news directors or managers will be friendly. Some won't. Some will be personable. Some will be all business. Mostly, they're looking for someone with confidence who can do the job *and* will fit into their newsroom. Some will stick to your experience only. Others may get more personal, asking you about work or journalism philosophy, what kind of people you like to work with, and so on. One reporter took his tape to two stations in a small market. They were literally right across the street. One news director told him she really liked his writing, but that he looked too young . . . call back next year. Across the street, that news director told him his look was great, but his writing really needed help! It can be frustrating, but realize you can't be all things to all news managers.

If you're getting a bad vibe from a news director, it probably means you don't want to work there in the first place. But be fair, too. Most news directors will be in a hurry. Don't mistake that for curtness or rudeness. You're just part of the job they have to do, and they have plenty to do, whether they're in a small market or one at the top. Always be polite and respectful, even if that person isn't your cup of tea. You never know, one day that news director may remember you and recommend you to another news director in a different market. It's happened before. The time to keep those burning bridges intact is the minute you start interning. What goes around comes around, especially in a business as small as this one. The key here is how you are treated by this particular person. They may be in a hurry, but are they listening to you, giving you some respect, too? If they are condescending, instead of advising, and that bothers you, this may not be the place for you. Remember, your first job is critical. You'll be learning here as never before. If you'll be just a warm body filling a space, instead of someone whose opinion and hard work counts, then it's probably better to pass and wait for the right job, where you'll be able to grow instead of wear yourself out.

With time, patience, and persistence, you'll find the job that fits you pretty well. When you do that, get to work, reread this book, and work your way up to the next market. Good luck.

18

WRAP-UP

And finally . . .

Don't sell yourself short. You *will* be overwhelmed, you *will* have a huge learning curve, and you *will* do things to make yourself look stupid. In the words of a very wise person who has now passed on, "If you knew everything before you started the job, you'd be the boss. If you don't make mistakes, you won't learn anything, and this job isn't for you." Of course, it never hurts to shorten that learning curve and make small mistakes, not the huge humdingers that news legends are made of.

A love of learning is key. Almost everyone we interviewed for this book said "learning something new every day" is what keeps them motivated day in and day out. It's what TV journalism is all about. The job may be a grind at times, but it is never boring. Develop confidence in yourself; you'll need it because you won't know everything. You can't. It's impossible to know everything about every story. Especially in a world that moves so fast and changes as quickly as ours does. Get used to change, learn about it, and love it.

News is really a labor of love. Most of us don't make the big bucks, have the cushy perks, work 9 to 5, or spend as much time with our families as we would like. It is a personal sacrifice. But you'll never be bored, and you'll laugh, cry, and scream on a weekly basis. You'll expand your horizons constantly. How many corporate types can say that? You'll go places, see things, meet people you've never dreamed of.

That's why we felt compelled to write this book. On a daily basis, your job may seem much worse, much more stressful than you'd thought it would be . . . but for a long-term career, it's much, much better, more exciting, more satisfying, than you would ever have believed it to be. You're compelled to do the best job you can every day; after all, your work will be exhibited before thousands of people, whether you're in front of or behind the camera. It's a sure performance enhancer. And at the end of every day, you'll know you affected those same thousands in some way.

Not many people can say that. Now, take a deep breath, smile, laugh, and get going!

Incidentally, this career will change you as a person, too. You'll see things, awful things, tragic things, beautiful things, secret things. You can't help but become less sensitized to certain things, like murder scenes. But since you see these things firsthand, you gain a heightened sensitivity. No, this crime isn't something I just saw on TV, I saw it with my own eyes, talked to the victim's family. They are real. You will meet people in power. You will meet famous people. You'll meet someone who's dying of a terrible degenerative disease, and you'll never forget him. Sometimes it's easy to lose sight of why journalists do their jobs every day. But what it really comes down to is meeting people, people who share the same physical world we do yet live in completely different ways than we do. And it's our job to tell their stories, whether we are assignment editors, producers, reporters, or photographers; it's up to us to give others a glimpse into the world we were privileged to see. Take a look and see for yourself.

READY, SET, GO!

It's time to make it happen. It's up to you. So, on the road to whatever your news future holds, keep these wrap-up Newsbite nuggets close by to help you navigate the best course for you. Good luck.

Dedication

"I would ride my bike a couple of miles a day in the scorching heat, to the station where I would learn to make beat calls, write, edit video, shoot, and report. It was the most fantastic experience. I offered to do everything and the news director let me."

Hayley Herst, executive producer

"Get in and take any job, then work your way through the system. Find a mentor who will put their arm around you and say, 'I'm gonna tell you something here, kid.'"

Patti Dennis, news director

Hard Work

"Be ready to dedicate your life to the cause. A reporter's job never ends."

Dan Lothian, correspondent, NBC

Signature Style

"A great photographer is someone who can take the boring, the mundane, and make it compelling, can personalize it, and make people care."

Eric Kehe, photographer

"I think the biggest challenge is trying to create 'pieces of art' every day and battling producers for that extra ten seconds needed to tell the story."

Sarah Pooler, former reporter/anchor

Thick Skin

"You can't take yourself too seriously. It is not about making the mistake but more how you recover from it. I lost way too much sleep for missing my first slot as a reporter or stumbling during a newscast as an anchor. You are a work in progress. Just work hard and you will grow and improve as a journalist."

Debbie Denmon, anchor

"A sense of humor is the most important thing. You'd better be able to laugh at yourself because hundreds of thousands of people will laugh at you when you choke on the air (and everyone does)."

Sarah Pooler, former reporter/anchor

"Roll with the punches, be very flexible. This business will chew you up and spit you out. Also, don't take it personally. If you are let go from a station, it may have nothing to do with you. When new management comes into a station, they have to make decisions. There will be casualties and sometimes that casualty will be you. In other words, don't put your suitcase too far back in the closet."

Juan Fernandez, reporter

Working Knowledge

"Seek quality employers. Work for good people at great stations regardless of market size and pay and you will be generally happy and your career will prosper. But, also, choose places where you want to live. If you're miserable fifteen hours a day it doesn't matter how good life is the other nine."

Jim Hanchett, anchor

"You're not special just because someone puts you in front of a camera to tell a story. You're only part of a team of professionals who are really at the service of the story. Get your head out of the clouds and concentrate on getting to the truth of the stories you're covering. Your face should never make the news. Your insights should."

Michael Moffett, freelance producer

"Everyone is under a deadline, so at times people seem to get a little stressed out. Remember, it is only TV. It's not brain surgery. You will probably have three more shows tomorrow to get it right."

Scott Jordon, videotape editor

Life Lesson

"In this business you will meet some of the most wonderful people and some of the most difficult people. You must realize that just because someone doesn't agree with you, doesn't mean they are stupid, stubborn, or mean. We all look at life differently. And, what one person sees as being stubborn, another might admire as being tenacious. Be flexible when working with dynamic personalities. It can help you survive in the world of TV news and life in general."

Tom Hanson, anchor

APPENDIX A: GOING ONLINE

Here's a "short list" of websites that we found to help you out. Anyone who's spent any time in cyberspace knows there is a lot out there about TV news jobs, whether it's getting them, or just talking about "the biz." Many of these websites have other links that are too numerous to mention here. They're easy to use, informative, and helpful. Log on.

Perhaps the best website we found was www.newslab.org. This site offers fresh ways to cover unexciting stories, and web resources to help you out with those stories, links to all kinds of sites, such as criminal justice resources, tips about how to do your job more effectively, and interesting articles of all kinds.

> www.ojr.org—Online Journalism Review
> emonline.com—Electronic Media's website
> assignmenteditor.com—Many of the links listed on this site require subscriptions.
> rtnda.com—The Radio and Television News Director's Association's website includes job listings, as do:
>> tvjobs.com
>> lostremote.com/jobs
>> journalismjobs.com
>> tvnewz.com
>> tvspy.com
> spyman.com/laws is a site that updates you on laws regarding what is legal to tape and what isn't.

A place to go for salary and cost of living information is home-fair.com, to see how expensive it is to live in various cities.

There are so many resources on the web (or the hard copy, for that matter) to read up on issues and current events, that it's impossible to list even a small percentage of them. But here goes:

newslink.org lists dozens of websites for newspapers and magazines; you basically select whatever you want.

Ipl.org/div/news is the Internet public library. You can look up just about any newspaper in the world. Want to find out what's going on today in Florence, Italy? Check it out.

Nytimes.com is the *New York Times* website. Always a great source of information for world, business, financial, and current events news.

Same for csmonitor.com—the *Christian Science Monitor*.

Kolisrael.com lists numerous websites to find out about Middle East issues from the mid-east point of view.

Theatlantic.com is the *Atlantic Monthly* magazine's website.

For state governments, type in "state government" in your search engine of choice, and a list of all the states' official websites, plus more, comes up.

Businessnation.com is an interesting site that lists business stories (which oftentimes can be hard to understand), business trends, and links to local business and economy issues in your state.

And you can never go wrong with the wallstreetjournal.com. (Subscription required, I think.) It's full of business news, current events, and just great nuggets of knowledge.

The key here, as with anything, is to be aware of the bias of the particular sites, and who's sponsoring them. They all offer certain points of view—liberal, conservative, business-oriented, and so on. Staying informed is the key, and with all these sites and more, there's no reason not to. Put some on your favorites page, then click on them when you have some down time. Get familiar with all kinds of places to go for all kinds of stories you may do—business, financial, government, political, investigative, you name it. Then you'll be able to look up good information in a pinch, under pressure.

Of course, any of these websites are subject to change. Use them, often, to help you get your job, to help you in your job, then again to help you find the next job.

A book you'll never want to be without in the newsroom is the *AP Stylebook:*

International Headquarters
50 Rockefeller Plaza
New York, NY 10020
www.ap.org

SOME OTHER GOOD BOOKS WITH NO-NONSENSE WRITING TIPS ARE:

Writing Broadcast News
Shorter, Sharper, Stronger
Mervin Block
Bonus Books
160 East Illinois Street
Chicago, IL 60611

Rewriting Network News
Mervin Block
Bonus Books
160 East Illinois Street
Chicago, IL 60611

And, of course, good old-fashioned periodicals, online, from the library, or with a subscription, will help broaden your horizons:

USA Today
Newsweek
Time
US News and World Report

And, tune into some news from around the world. The BBC "World Report," on radio or television, is interesting because you get a view of news from outside our nation. National Public Radio can give you some news that you probably won't hear or see anywhere else. And check out solid documentary news programs like "Frontline" and "CloseUp" on your local PBS station.

APPENDIX B: ABOUT THE
JOURNALISTS INTERVIEWED

Thanks to all of those hard-working journalists who shared their insights with us. Here's a little bit about their careers:

Chris Berg, reporter/weekend assignment editor, KRDO-TV, Colorado Springs, Colorado; assignment editor, KMGH-TV, Denver; news director, KOB-TV, Albuquerque, New Mexico; news director, KSTP, Minneapolis, Minnesota

Erin Crowley, producer, KDVR Fox31 News, Denver; MSNBC; KUSA, Denver; KGW, Portland, Oregon; WKRN, Nashville, Tennessee; WCSH, Portland, Maine; WLBZ, Bangor, Maine

Debbie Denmon, news anchor, WFAA-TV, Dallas, Texas. "I anchor morning and midday news shows, anchoring four hours a day. This is my first full-time anchor gig. I was weekend anchor/reporter in Indianapolis for nearly three years at WTHR-TV and before that I spent three years as weekend anchor/reporter in Tulsa, Oklahoma, at KJRH-TV. I started in Colorado Springs, Colorado, and stayed there for nearly a year and a half, doing mainly reporting with some fill-in anchor experience."

Patti Dennis, vice president/news director, KUSA, Denver

Mona Dyer, assignment manager, Colorado Springs, Colorado; news director, Grand Junction, Colorado

Juan Fernandez, reporter, fill-in anchor, fill-in weather, Los Angeles; assignment editor, associate producer, field producer, reporter, Miami

Jim Hanchett, anchor, WECT-TV, Wilmington, North Carolina. "After college I worked as a newspaper reporter in Lawrence, Massachusetts, and in Denver; then as a reporter at KCNC-TV in Denver for twelve years; then as a correspondent for NBC news channel based in Denver and Washington."

Tom Hanson, anchor, Sioux Falls, South Dakota. Previously a production assistant; studio camera; master control operator; technical director; photographer; fill-in sports anchor; morning weather; news reporter; news producer in markets including Rapid City, South Dakota; Colorado Springs, Colorado; Salt Lake City, Utah; Sioux Falls, South Dakota

Sarah Harlow, formerly reporter/anchor KSDK TV St. Louis, held similar positions at KUTV Utah; WDEF Chattanooga; and WMDT Salisbury, Maryland

Hayley Herst, executive producer, KDVR Fox31 News, Denver; news director at KRNV, Reno, Nevada; videotape editor, field producer, morning producer, afternoon producer, executive producer, KVBC, Las Vegas

Eric Kehe, multi-award-winning photographer, director of photography, KUSA, Denver

Scott Jordon, videotape editor. "I have worked in two markets, Reno, market size 117, and San Diego, market size 26."

Dan Lothian, west coast correspondent, NBC News; reporter, WCVB-Boston; reporter, KING-TV Seattle; reporter, WPTV West Palm Beach; reporter, WDEF Chattanooga

Carol Lynde, videographer/editor, Phoenix; Atlanta; Great Falls, Montana; Denver

Michael Moffett, director of Camino Media, Madrid, Spain; producer/correspondent in Iberia for "National Geographic Today," Euronews, Discovery, PBS/Deutsche Welle TV Newsmagazine "European Journal"; videojournalist for Video News International (New York Times Television); contributing producer to APTN's "Roving Report"; reporter/anchor in Great Falls, Montana; Bakersfield, California; and Sarasota, Florida

Janine White, videotape editor, news photographer, Augusta, Georgia; photojournalist, Louisville, Kentucky; videotape editor, Denver

NEWS GLOSSARY

A-Block   The first section of the news before the commercial break. Hence, the B-block is the second section, and so on.

Add   When you need an extra story in the rundown, whether it's for time or for a spot news situation.

Anchor Wrap   A package with anchor voiceover. They didn't necessarily write the story, or it may even be a package taken from the satellite feed that the anchor re-voiced.

Ax   Accident; for example, *car ax* is a slug name.

Banner   Just like it sounds. A banner of information usually displayed at the bottom of the screen during a story. Usually used to emphasize a point, like "War on Terrorism," or "Light Rail Crash."

Beat Check/Beat Calls   Making calls to various agencies (police, fire, etc.) to check what's going on.

Box Shot   Shot of the anchor, slightly off-center, with a "box" or graphic in the corner, literally over their shoulder. The box illustrates what the story is about, like a gun or a freeze frame of the president. Also called **over-the-shoulder, or OTS.**

B-Roll   Video for VO.

CG   Stands for character generator. These are the words that appear on-screen during stories: people's names, locations, and so on. Example: John Smith, River City Water Board. Also called **font, chyron, super**.

Chyron   Also means character generator, or **CG, font, super.**

Cold Open   Any type of video, be it a VO, SOT, or natural sound, that runs right after the show open, before the anchors are on camera. Usually used when you have an exceptionally compelling piece of video that you want to use right off the top. Example: Show open: "River City's Best Newsteam, this is News 6 at 6." NATS up of an explosion, video continues rolling, anchors then talk over the video: "A suspicious package is detonated by the bomb squad, on a busy street corner" [anchors on camera]. "Good evening, I'm Jane Smith." "And I'm John Jacobs."

Comrex   The battery-powered receiver in which a reporter plugs the IFB.

Crawl   Words at the bottom of the screen that go from right to left, used to alert viewers about any breaking news, usually severe weather. This way viewers can be alerted to breaking news situations without interrupting programming.

Crosstalk   The anchors talking to each other about a story.

Cue   The GO signal a producer or floor director gives to a reporter or anchor.

Custom Live   Same as **generic live,** except one specific station gets to continue talking with the live reporter.

Cutline   A word or short phrase at the bottom of the OTS box, like *Shooting,* or *President Bush.*

Drop   This is when the producer deletes a story from the rundown, for one reason or another, usually if the newscast is "heavy" and there's not enough time for everything.

ETA   Estimated time of arrival, that is, how long it will take you to get back to the station.

Evergreen   A story that can run any time.

Feed   A video newswire a station subscribes to that comes down the same time every day, via satellite. If a station is part of a network, the network will provide this. And the station can add special services, like a health feed, with specifically health-related stories.

Feedback   Hearing your own voice in the IFB.

Filler   Additional stories, usually in the context that the show is light and needs an extra story or two to fill the time.

Float   When a story doesn't air in its "slot," for a variety of reasons, and the story has to be moved to another "slot," later on in the show, it "floats."

Fluff   Nonessential news, light fare.

Font   Stands for character generator, or **CG, chyron, super.**

Full   After the two-box shot, when the reporter shot is taken full screen.

Fullscreen   A graphic that covers the entire screen, that gives information, like a list of items, or a description of a suspect on the loose.

Full-Screen Tag   A voiceover tag, but not with video, with a full-screen graphic, usually a phone number. For example, *for more information, call 555–1111.* The producer usually is the one to order this from the graphics department.

Generic Live   When a network does one live shot at the top of the hour, and several affiliates pick it up at the same time.

GFX   Abbreviation for graphics.

Graphic   Any preproduced graphic depiction of information for a news story, like a mug shot or a map of where an incident has taken place.

Half-Screen   When the talent is positioned on one side of the screen, and information is on the other side, usually with a transparent graphic, to impart extra information. Also called **panel.**

Happy-Talk   Filler talk to fill the end of the show.

Heavy   A show that is short on time. Reporters and anchors will be asked to "keep it tight."

HFR   Hold for release. A package done previously, to be used at producer's discretion. Usually a feature story that can be run any time, it is great for slow news days.

HUT   Homes using television. Another percentage used in measuring ratings.

IFB   Interrupted feedback. Nontechnically, around the newsroom, it's a talent's earpiece. Technically, it's a means of communication between a reporter live on-scene and the producer back at the station where the producer is able to talk to the reporter (or an anchor on set) through an earpiece.

Incue   The one or two words the reporter says that give the director of the newscast the "cue" to roll video.

Intro   The written introduction to a package or a live shot. Usually read on-air by the anchor.

Kicker   The last story in the show, a "happy" story to end the show with.

Land Line   Call from a phone that's hard wired, like a pay phone, in places where a cell phone doesn't work.

Lav Mic   A lavaliere microphone; a small one that pins to the collar or coat.

Lead   The first and most important story of the day.

Lead-in   The first part of a package or live shot, which the anchor reads.

Light   A story short on content; reporters and anchors may have to "stretch" to fill time.

Live Shot   A reporter at the scene of a story reporting live.

Live Wraparound   A reporter is live at the scene of a story, tossing-to and tagging-out of a package. Hence the anchor tosses to the reporter, the reporter tosses to the package, the reporter then wraps up after the taped package, and tosses back to the anchor on-set.

Local Angle   Making a national story meaningful to local viewers. Many times this means finding someone in your viewing area whom the story affects.

Localize   Same as *local angle*.

Microwave Shot   A live shot utilizing a microwave truck or van. Most local live shots are via microwave. The signal is sent from the microwave truck to the station, or to a repeater signal, then to the station.

Mix-Minus   The term for when the audio engineer at the station filters out feedback from the IFB of a reporter doing a satellite live shot. If you don't have mix-minus, the reporter on the satellite live shot will hear his/her own voice in their earpiece, but delayed a few seconds; very distracting.

NATS   A piece of video that has natural sound on it, like water rushing for a flooding story. Gives the viewer a you-are-there feeling.

NATS Sound Full   Natural sound and video. Also called **NATS-VO.**

NATS-VO   Natural sound and video. Video with natural sound up full. Example: a story about a river would have the anchor reading on camera, the anchor would stop talking as the video rolls, and viewers hear the sound of the rushing water. The sound fades under, then the anchor continues on with the story as the video continues to roll.

Newsroom Live   When the reporter presents a story live from the newsroom.

Nightside   The staff that works the afternoon/evening shift.

On-Camera Tag   Just what this sounds like. Used after a package, or VO/SOT, it indicates to the anchor that they will be on-camera for the last part of the story. Important so the anchor will make sure to look on camera. Needs to be indicated on the script.

On-Set   A reporter doing his/her live shot from the anchor desk, instead of from a remote location.

Outcue   The last few words of a SOT, written on the script, so the director will know when to come back to anchors or reporter on camera.

Over-the-Shoulder   Shot of the anchor, slightly off-center, with a "box" or graphic in the corner, literally over their shoulder. The box illustrates what the story is about, like a gun or a freeze frame of the president. Also called **OTS** or **box shot.**

Package   See **PKG.**

Panel   When the talent is positioned on one side of the screen, and information is on the other side, usually with a transparent graphic, to impart extra information. Also called **half-screen.**

Peg   The angle of the story.

Phoner   A television news story reported over the telephone with or without VO or SOTs. A phoner is used most often when a live shot fails.

PIO   Public Information Officer. Designated person who gives information, usually at the scene of a crime or emergency.

PKG   Package. A full-length story written and voiced by a reporter. Includes VO and SOTs edited together with reporter voice track in between.

Pool   Video and sound of a story shot by one station in a market but shared by all. Usually used in a court or press conference situation to cut down on the number of cameras at one time.

Pre-Pro   Graphics or animation pre-produced for a **PKG** or for the show.

Preshow   The teases that run before the news starts, so viewers know what's coming up. Can contain either video, a soundbite, natural sound, or all three.

PSA   Public Service Announcement. This is a spot for a public interest purposes, like an anti-drug campaign, not paid for. Stations are required to run a certain number of these as a public service to the community.

PUT   Persons using television. Another factor in measuring the share.

Rating   A percentage of all television households.

Reader   A television news story read by the anchor on camera with no VO or SOTs.

Remote   A reporter live at a remote location.

Rundown   The blueprint of the newscast, listing each story in order, who reads it, and everything else about what is happening in literally every second of the newscast.

Sat Shot   A live shot utilizing a satellite truck or van. Usually for live shots that are too far away or inaccessible for a microwave signal. The signal is sent up to a satellite, then sent back down, and picked up at the station.

Scanner Traffic   Things you hear on the scanner.

Share   The percentage of television households watching a particular program.

Show & Tell   When a reporter uses a prop or action to illustrate something in a **PKG** or live shot.

Slot   Where a story falls in the rundown, i.e., airs in the show. If you "miss slot," you missed air, unless the producer can shuffle you into another "slot."

Slug   Story name.

SOT   Sound on tape or a soundbite. Basically, an interview that is taped and run on air. Sometimes just called "sound."

Soundbite/Bite   Same as **SOT,** or sound on tape.

Special Feed   During spot news situations, networks or news services may set up separate feeds for video, so the subscriber stations can get video right away. Generally coordinated by assignment editor or producer, along with engineering.

Spot News   Breaking news situations, news that's happening right now.

SPX   Abbreviation for sports in the rundown.

Squeezeback   When the picture on the screen is made small, i.e., squeezed, to accommodate other information, like a weather crawl at the bottom of the screen.

Stand-up   The on-camera portion of the reporter in a package.

Stick Mic   The handheld microphone.

Still   One frame of video, used as a box, or a background for a graphic, like a still frame of a huge wall of fire, used as a background under information about the fire, such as how many homes destroyed, etc.

Straight Live   No package, no VO, no SOTs. Just the reporter, live, from the scene of the story, standing and talking on-camera the entire time.

Straight PKG   A full-length television news story aired without a reporter live shot. Ends with reporter tag, for example, "In River City, I'm John Smith, News 13."

Tag   Like the introduction only at the end of the **PKG,** usually read by the anchor on camera. It could also be thought of as the end of the story.

Talent   On-air personalities.

Talk Back   When the anchors interview someone other than the reporter live, on-scene of a story. This is a very common format on the Sunday morning news shows, or "Nightline," when Ted Koppel sits in the studio, then interviews people from around the world live.

Team Coverage   During a huge news story with many angles, many reporters work on different parts of the same story, introduced as team coverage, so viewers know there are many stories about the larger issue (for example, a forest fire: one reporter at the scene doing the straight fire coverage, another reporter at a shelter for displaced homeowners, another reporter with investigators, nailing down how the fire started, the weather person with the forecast to report if the weather will cooperate, and so on).

Tease   After each block, the stories that are coming up. Very important, and truly a skill to write, to keep viewers interested.

Toss   When an anchor introduces a reporter for a live shot or when a reporter introduces a story in a live shot. A kind of intro to another reporter or to a piece of tape.

TRT   Total running time, i.e., of a SOT, written on the script, so that director will know when to come back to camera.

Two-Box   When the anchor introduces a live shot, and the anchor is in one "box," and the reporter is on the other side of the screen in another "box."

VO   Voiceover. An anchor or reporter "voices over" video. The talent isn't on screen, just the video. Also called **b-roll.**

VO/SOT   Voiceover–sound on tape. A television news story read by the anchor, video rolling on screen, followed by a sound bite. One of the most common forms of stories in a newscast.

Wrap   The *stop* signal a producer or floor director gives to a reporter or anchor.

WX   Abbreviation for Weather in the rundown.

INDEX

Page numbers followed by *b, f,* or *t* refer to blocked text, figures, and tables respectively.

advertising, 63. *See also* sales department

anchor, 30, 66; tips, 156–58

assignment editor: responsibilities, 31–32; scenarios, 22–23, 33, 135–41; tips, 11, 19–20, 92–93, 114–15, 159

assistant news director, 31

Berg, Chris, 2*b,* 4*b*

"books," 62–63, 66. *See also* ratings period

bottom line, 59–60. *See also* sales department

camera equipment, 81–84, 82*t;* legal issues, 104–5

clerk of council, 102

clerk of court, 100

clothes, 18–19

Columbine incident, 75–76

common mistakes, 6–8, 153–60; anchors, 156–58; assignment editors, 159; photographers, 159–60; producers, 155–56; writers, 125–27, 153–55

contact list, 12, 53, 89–91

convergence, 67–69

cop shop, 101–2

court, 100–101, 101*t. See also* legal issues

criticism, 51–52

cross-promotion, 65–66. *See also* sales department

Crowley, Erin, 9*b,* 35*b,* 45*b,* 119*b*

danger, 26–27, 26*b*

deadline, 113–18

Denmon, Debbie, xiii, 17*b,* 33*b,* 153*b,* 167

Dennis, Patti, 1*b,* 76*b,* 167

district attorney, 102

Dotson, Bob, 130

Dyer, Mona, 71*b*

editor, tips, 20–21

engineering department, 39

ethics, 71–72, 74–78
exclusive information, 52

flow, 96–97

general manager (GM), 30–31
golden triangle, 64
government, 102–3

Hanchett, Jim, xiii, 168
Hanson, Tom, xii, 61*b*, 169
Hernandez, Juan, 7*b*, 158*b*, 168
Herst, Hayley, 5*b*, 45*b*, 78*b*, 166–67
hospital, 103–4

information overload, 86–89
internship, 84
interview, 91–93; legal issues, 105–7;
    of victim, 75–78

job hunting, 161–64
job performance feedback, 48, 51–52
Jordon, Scott, xiii, 168

Kehe, Eric, 37*b*, 48*b*, 79*b*, 167
knowledge, importance of, 143–46

legal issues, 104–9; interview, 105–7;
    music and movie clips, 109;
    slander, 108; video and hidden
    cameras, 104–5
live shot, 35, 95–96
local government, 102
Lothian, Dan, xiv, 26*b*, 167
Lynde, Carol, xiii, 75*b*, 82*b*, 151

management, 30–31
managing editor, 31
media conglomerates, 9–10

Moffett, Michael, xiv, 168
movie clip, 109
music clip, 109
myths, 1–2

networking, 53
news director, 31, 161–64
newsroom: chaos in, 2–3, 17–18;
    hierarchy, 29–31, 29*f;* survival kit,
    18*b*
newsroom survival guide, 43–56;
    exclusive information, 52; filing
    story ideas, 47–48; job
    performance feedback, 48, 51–52;
    pressure, 50–51; respect for others,
    43–47; rundown, 53–56; team
    approach, 49. *See also* contact list
news station, 9–12; business
    influence, 59–60; market pulse,
    11–12; newscast styles, 10–11;
    ownership, 9–10

O-A-A (Observe-Absorb-Ask), 21–22
objectivity, 71–72
one-man band, 79–81
on-set piece, 35
overnights, 62

packaging, 35, 93–95
pay, xiii, 61, 61*b*
payola agreement, 75
perks, xii–xiii, xiv, 165–66
phoner, 106–7, 149. *See also*
    interviews
photographer: responsibilities, 36–37;
    scenarios, 23–24, 135–41; tips, 12,
    20–21, 92, 159–60
PIO (public information officer), 23*b*,
    99, 102

"plugola" agreement, 75
Pooler, Sarah, xiii, 167, 168
pressure, 50–51
producer: common mistakes, 155–56;
    responsibilities, 34–35; scenarios,
    24–25, 135–41; tips, 11–12, 20,
    93, 114–15
production department, 38
promotions department, 39
public affairs department, 39
public information officer. *See* PIO
    (public information officer)

ratings, 10
ratings period, 59, 62–64, 66
reporter: responsibilities, 35–36;
    scenarios, 24–25, 73, 109–10,
    135–41
reporter, tips, 12, 20, 86–93, 114–15;
    contact list, 12, 53, 89–91; inter-
    view, 75–78, 91–93; organizing
    information, 86–89
rundown, 53–56, 54*t*

salary, xiii, 61, 61*b*
sales department, 39, 59, 65–66
slander, 108
"slow news day," 47–48
stand-up, 95
state government, 103
station. *See* news station

statistics, 129
story, 85–98; contact list, 89–91;
    flow, 96–97; information overload,
    86–89; interview, 91–93; live shot,
    95–96; packaging, 93–95; team
    approach, 97–98
success, recipe for, 3–6
sweeps, 62–63. *See also* ratings
    period

talent, 30, 66; tips, 156–58
Tallman, Jacki, 99*b*, 104*b*
team approach, 49, 97–98, 110–11
teases, 130–31, 155
technological convergence, 67–69
timecode, 116

video, legal issues, 104–5
VO (voice over) sample, 20*b*

Wall Street Journal, 146
White, Janine, xiii
WIIFM (what's in it for me?), 88,
    119–20
worst-case scenario, 147–51
wraparound live shot, 35
writing tips, 94–95, 119–31; basics,
    120–25; common mistakes,
    125–27, 153–55; perspective,
    128–29; teases, 130–31; WIIFM,
    119–20

ABOUT THE AUTHORS

Robert Thompson is an award-winning reporter/anchor with fifteen years on-air experience. He has covered the gamut of stories from the Oklahoma City bombing case to the Academy of Country Music Awards. His goal in coauthoring this book is to arm readers with knowledge that will help them survive and thrive in the evolving world of TV news. He has a degree in speech communications from Colorado State University.

Cindy Malone is an Emmy award–winning news producer and former television news reporter and anchor. Her career spans more than a decade, coast to coast. She and her husband own their own multi-award-winning television production company, and consider having one of their videos in the Smithsonian Institution to be one of their highest achievements. She has a degree in technical journalism with a concentration in business from Colorado State University.